Healing Guides

Witchcraft

THE MODERN BOOK
OF MAGIC

SparkPool

INTRODUCTION

What images spring to mind when you think about witchcraft, or when you hear the word 'witch'? Do you conjure up images of ancient crones flying on broomsticks, with tall pointed hats, flapping black capes and hooked noses? Perhaps you see cauldrons, cats, and double, double, toil and trouble? While deeply ingrained in our collective consciousness, those images are outdated, out of sync with the modern world and a little radical! It's time to replace them with pictures of powerful men and women, working potent magic – and not a cape, broomstick or hooked nose in sight (but maybe still a cat or two!).

In the modern world, witchcraft has taken on a vibrant new look, a fresh feel and a positive purpose, and it's one that more and more people are exploring to enhance their lives. Today, people around the world are reclaiming skills that possess an ancient history. These modern-day witches are turning to crystals, herbs and spells. They are embracing non-traditional forms of spirituality, and utilising underestimated skills of intuition and emotional intelligence. This is witchcraft in its purest form.

Witches and history

In its true sense, witchcraft is a collection of beliefs in the supernatural that dates back centuries, if not thousands of years. It includes traditions and practices that involve using magic to bring about desired outcomes. In witchcraft, magic takes its form in the use of rituals, herbs, crystals, chants and other methods to tap into a universal power and utilise it.

In times gone by, those who used herbs and plants to bring about change held powerful positions in society. They were healers, who used their knowledge to help others. These people were often revered and respected in the societies in which they lived. As times changed, people found it difficult to understand these ancient practices and the healers of communities became known as 'witches', and their work was labelled as 'witchcraft'. Those accused of such a craft were often persecuted for their beliefs.

Witches today

Thankfully, contemporary cultures are far more accepting. There is now recognition that magic can be used to improve the life of the user, and the lives of others. Modern-day witches are reviving the true aim of witchcraft, and dispelling its tarnished historical reputation. People everywhere are practising this powerful and potent magic. Their aim is to bring positivity to the world, creating events and outcomes that are widely beneficial. They seek to act in harmony with universal energy, utilising this powerful source to bring about only good. They use that energy to enhance their careers, their relationships, their economic power, their homes, their wellbeing and more. They desire to be empowered, enriched individuals who exert a positive control and influence over their lives. Sounds exciting, purposeful and powerful? Sounds like witchcraft!

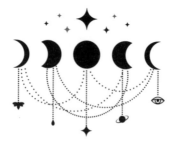

HOW TO USE THIS BOOK

So, if you are interested in witchcraft and what it could do for you, get set to tap into this enriching world. This book will help you to discover how you can use your natural talents to improve your life. You'll learn how to manifest an improvement to your finances, your health, your relationships and much more. You'll also discover how you can help others. By connecting to your own spirituality and inner power, you'll be able to bring about change that will benefit not only yourself, but those around you too.

Steadily spellbound

We suggest reading through the book first, before you set out to perform any spells. This will ensure you have everything you need and that you understand the basics of magic before getting started. Start with a few simple spells to ease you into things, then move on as you grow in confidence. Every witch learns along the way, and the process of learning is all part of your journey. Before you know it, you'll be making magic and discovering just how powerful you really are!

Note: This book requires the use of essential oils, candles, smudging and general use of open flames. Always use essential oils with care and consult a doctor if you suffer from any adverse effects. Please exercise caution when using open flames and ensure lit candles are never left unattended. When smudging or burning other items during spells, keep a fireproof tray or plate to hand and keep a close eye on them. Happy casting!

A witch's tools

In this book, you will use spells, rituals, crystals and much more to make magic. You can easily find all of the equipment you will need online or in local shops. Below is a list of what to stock up on before we get started.

You will need:

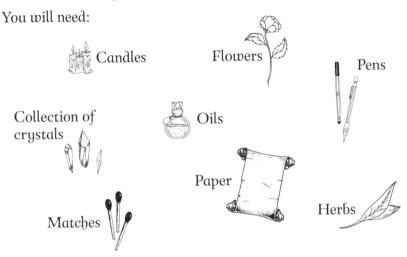

Candles

Flowers

Pens

Collection of crystals

Oils

Paper

Herbs

Matches

GOOD TO KNOW

Venturing into witchcraft is exciting – you'll discover a wonderful world full of amazing possibilities. However, as you do so, you may also discover that some people aren't as positive about your newfound powers if you mention them! In those instances, it helps to have some useful myth-busting points to dust off any doubters. If you're asked if you have a penchant for brooms, say yours is strictly for sweeping the kitchen floor. You don't frolic with the Devil on a Friday evening over a bottle of wine, nor does your saucepan double up as a cauldron. You might wear black simply because it goes with everything – and your pet cat is simply your cute sidekick!

THE WITCH'S PANTRY

Any witch worth their salt, if you'll pardon the pun, has a pantry stocked with magical herbs, spices, incense and oils, ready to use in a variety of spells and potions. But before you stock up your witch's pantry, it's helpful to get to know the energy behind the different ingredients you'll be using. Learning about the natural magic and healing powers of plants, herbs and oils is both fascinating and empowering. There isn't space to mention all of them, but here are some you might find most useful and effective.

Herbs and other botanicals

When you come across a spell which requires ingredients such as 'botanicals', this just means a plant or a plant part, like flowers, leaves, seeds, stems, roots etc. Herbs are plants such as rosemary, parsley and so on, which are used for their flavour as well as their magical or medicinal properties. Here are a few botanicals and herbs you'll find in this book, along with their major properties.

- **Bay:** for strength and prophetic dreams
- **Camomile:** promotes inner peace, eases rage and heightened sensitivity, and invites luck and love
- **Cinnamon:** use for love, passion, prosperity, personal strength and psychic awareness
- **Cumin:** good for healing, protection, love, lust, new beginnings and emotional strength
- **Garlic:** use for protection, strength and healing

- **Ginger:** use for healing, protection, luck, passion and spell enhancement
- **Lavender:** use for happiness, strengthening relationships, inner strength, psychic power, peace and meditation
- **Rosemary:** use for its strong protective and cleansing powers
- **Sage:** use for wisdom, wishes, knowledge, strength, cleansing and vitality
- **Thyme:** use for strength, courage, wisdom and willpower in difficult situations

Essential oils

Essential oils are highly concentrated extracts of flowers, herbs, roots or resin extract, sometimes diluted in neutral-base oil. They're commonly used to anoint tools that are used in spells and rituals, such as candles and crystals. Some witches even use them to anoint their own bodies. Take care with oils and avoid using them around your eyes. It's a good idea to keep clean cotton gloves in your witch's kitchen for handling sensitive materials.

- **Eucalyptus oil:** invokes calmness, improves concentration and promotes balance and healing
- **Mint oil:** cleansing and motivational
- **Geranium oil:** helps to decrease stress and balance emotions while calming and restoring inner peace
- **Clove oil:** protection, cleansing, spiritual healing and spell enhancement
- **Rose oil:** inspires emotional calm and stability
- **Peppermint oil:** helps to soothe the nerves, focus the senses and stimulate alertness

Incense

Incense is a substance that contains fragrant herbs, flowers, resins, gums and wood chips, infused with pure essential oils that you burn to release their scent. You can buy different blends of incense for different magical purposes, like a protection incense to drive away negative energies. You can also make your own blends. Turn the page to read about the properties of some of the incense used in this book.

- **Sandalwood:** decreases anxiety, calms the nervous system and helps you sleep better
- **Dragon's blood:** use for protection, cleansing, purifying and strengthening
- **Frankincense:** reduces stress, helping to improve your mood and your concentration
- **Ylang-ylang:** enhances your inner confidence, filling you with warmth and joy
- **Patchouli:** known for being sensual, grounding and alluring

Store them up

If you buy your herbs and spices in plastic or paper bags, transfer them to glass storage jars or containers. You can decorate the labels you put on the jars to make it easier to locate the one you need and to make them look beautiful and unique to you! But using old, recycled jam jars works just as well. Just make sure the jars are completely clean and dry before filling them. Daylight can affect botanicals and oils, so it's best to keep them in a special cupboard, cabinet or box. Just make sure your essential oils are kept on a different shelf or section and cannot tip over and soak your other ingredients.

GOOD TO KNOW

Smudge sticks are bundles of herbs tied together by twine. After setting fire to a smudge stick, let it burn for about 20 seconds, then gently blow out the flame so you can see orange embers. Burning herbs in this way can cleanse a person, space or object of negative energy.

THE MAGIC IN COLOUR AND DAYS

You're already more of a witch than you know! You regularly use colour magic without even noticing it. You know how good it feels to bask in the Sun? You're connecting with the magical powers of yellow and gold. It's also the reason that looking at a blue ocean might make us feel calm. In magic, colours and days have powers that can inform all of your spells and even your day-to-day life.

To fully tune in to the power of colours, you need to know a bit more about their meanings. Then, you're all set to surround yourself with some colour magic.

The power of colour

These are the general meanings that colours hold, and what they represent magically, but we all relate to colours in different ways, so you may want to experiment to see what feels right for you.

- **Red:** for strong emotions, courage, passion and strength
- **Orange:** for energy, attraction, vibrancy and motivation
- **Yellow:** for inspiration, imagination and knowledge
- **Green:** for growth, wealth, renewal, luck and balance
- **Blue:** for calm, truth, wisdom and protection
- **Purple:** for spirituality, wisdom, devotion, peace and idealism

- **White:** for peace, innocence, understanding and purity
- **Black:** for dignity, force, stability, protection and repels negativity
- **Gold:** for inner strength, self-realisation, understanding, good fortune and intuition
- **Silver:** for wisdom, psychic ability, intelligence and memory
- **Pink:** for nurturing, emotional healing and harmony

Work those colours!

You can use colour magic to great effect in the paint or fabrics you choose for your home, in the flowers you buy, the clothes you wear or even the food you eat!

So, if you're feeling a little vulnerable, throw on some black garments. Black is the colour of protection and will banish negative energy and make you feel safer. Feeling a bit flat and in need of an injection of joy and pleasure in your everyday life? Place an orange throw on your bed and soak up those good vibes each time you lie on it. Red is the colour of passion, so reach for that crimson lipstick next time you have a hot date. Green is a good colour for luck, so why not add some green nail polish to ensure that date goes well!

Days of magic

Each of the seven days of the week carries its own magical energy. Each day is also linked to different colours. Learning these connections can help you choose the most auspicious time and colours to practise magic!

- **Monday** is linked to silver, white and blue: peace, beauty, sleep, dreams, emotions, travel, fertility, insight and wisdom
- **Tuesday** is linked to red, black and orange: courage, strength, success, self-belief, rebellion and self-defence
- **Wednesday** is linked to purple and orange: communication, creativity, change and good fortune
- **Thursday** is linked to blue and green: abundance, protection, strength, wealth and healing
- **Friday** is linked to pink and aqua: love, birth, fertility, romance, gentleness and friendship
- **Saturday** is linked to black and purple: banishing, protection, wisdom, spirituality and cleansing
- **Sunday** is linked to gold and yellow: success, promotion, wealth and prosperity

SETTING YOUR ALTAR/ CREATING SACRED SPACES

Every witch needs an altar of their own. An altar is a place, however small, that's yours and yours alone. It's a sacred space where you can go for healing, inspiration, spiritual rituals, spellwork or just to recentre yourself after a stressful day. An altar is a place to put all your favourite meaningful and magical items on display, ready for enchantment any time they're needed. The size and shape of your altar don't matter – what matters is it's your space and you feel good in it. So don't delay – sort out your altar today!

An altar of your own

Setting up an altar shouldn't be too difficult. First, choose a piece of furniture to use as an altar. Repurpose or buy a second-hand table or cabinet. You could also use a small wall shelf, bedside table or even a windowsill as an altar. Some people have a permanent altar, while others who have limited space might use a drawer or a shelf on a bookcase. If space is really tight, find a box to keep your magical objects safe and private, and take them out and place them on top of the box when in use. Most importantly, make sure you can sit comfortably and quietly at your altar.

When it comes to choosing where to put your altar, trust your instincts. Where do you feel most present, spiritually connected and content? Try some different options. When a space feels right, you'll just know it in your witchy bones! Your altar can be anywhere. It can be indoors or outdoors. You could choose a table in a green space outside in nature, or carry out a box of altar items when you need to. Or you can place your altar in a permanent special place, like a bedroom that is quiet, dimly lit and easy to relax in. An altar is personal to you, and it may change as you change, so if you feel like changing or moving your altar after a while, go for it. There's no right or wrong way to make or place an altar – it's your space, and only yours.

Sacred set–ups

Now for the really fun part – setting up your altar. Let's say you have opted for a table altar: how should you place your items on it for maximum witchy wondrousness? Witches believe that it's important to incorporate the four elements of the universe that are essential to life – Earth, Air, Water and Fire – into their practice. These four elements control the weather, life and the development of every living thing on earth. So, try to include things that symbolise these four elements on your altar. For example, you could have stones, plants or flowers to represent Earth; candles, incense or oil burners to represent Fire; a bowl of water, seashells or sea glass to represent Water and a feather, wind chimes or a diffuser to represent Air. The elements are also linked to different directions, so place the groups of items you choose at the points of the compass on your altar. Items linked to the Earth element should sit at north, Air at east, Fire at south and Water at west.

Own it!

Don't stop there... use your imagination and add some flair! Choose other meaningful altar items to add to your collection. You can add anything that holds significance to you such as jewellery, charms or books. You could hang a witch's ladder for good energy and protection above the altar (more on this on page 67), or drape fabric of a particular colour over the surface. You might want to refresh your altar on the changing of the seasons or on sabbat days*. You may also need a small cabinet or box for herbs and oils and other objects you want to use in rituals.

*Sabbat days are seasonal festivals observed by witches throughout the year, which usually consist of the main solar events and the mid-points between them. They celebrate the Earth's trips around the Sun.

CHARMS, TALISMANS, AFFIRMATIONS, INCANTATIONS

Your treasure trove of magical and meaningful resources doesn't have to be limited to your altar. There are many other spellbinding objects and activities you can add to your witchy box of tricks. They can also be words, feelings and thoughts that can bring about change in the physical world too.

Charmed, I'm sure...

From four-leaf clovers to dice and horseshoes, lots of different things are traditionally used by people as lucky charms. A charm is an object that represents a change or result that you desire. Charms are usually worn or carried. They don't have to be worn in plain sight, like a brooch; they can simply be carried in a pouch or purse or worn under clothes. Charms can also be left in the home or other space, for example, to expel bad vibes or to be used when making magic. Charms help to focus the mind and direct energy to help make the desired change happen. Some people divide charms into amulets and talismans.

- An amulet is a natural object found by accident or deliberately collected or bought to be used as a charm. Amulets can be things like stones, crystals, fossils, bird feathers, four-leaf clovers, pieces of wood, nuts, shells, dried flowers or other herbs and seeds. You can choose any object that speaks to you for an amulet.

- A talisman is a human-made object used as a charm. Some talismans are carried by their owners at all times, often worn on a chain around the neck. Talismans may be made from materials found in nature, but these materials are always used to make a human-made design and usually incorporate words or symbols. The words and symbols echo the wearer's magical goals. A talisman may be a shaped piece of metal, wood, stone or paper that has words, symbols or objects etched, engraved, carved, painted, printed or stuck onto it. A pentacle is a star shaped symbol, believed to have magical properties and is often used in talismans.

In addition to charms, many witches also own jewellery, crystals, gemstones or other items that give them luck, hope and positive energy or help them work their magic. Some people hang bells or chimes outside their homes to ward off negative energy and prevent it from entering their home. Almost any object can become a charm, as long as it means something to you and helps you to channel your energy to the world around you.

Affirmative!

And that brings us neatly on to affirmations! So much of what you'll do as a witch will come down to confidence and belief. And that's where affirmations come in. Affirmations are powerful phrases you write down or memorise and then read out loud and repeat. They can be life-changing. To choose a phrase, think about who you are, how you feel and who you want to be. Choose a phrase that will help you achieve your goals, such as: "I am a strong, independent person"; "I can achieve anything I set out to do" or "I am letting go of the past". Looking in the mirror while you recite affirmations can feel really empowering. You may have to give it more than one shot. At first, repeating a phrase to yourself over and over again might feel strange, silly or even like a waste of time. Rest assured, it isn't. Words are powerful and affirmations can really help you harness the power of positive thinking and mindfulness and channel your inner energy.

Incantations

Affirmations also help you warm up those vocal cords and develop your belief in the power of words in preparation for learning incantations. An incantation is a spell created by using words. An incantation can be spoken, sung or chanted, and is intended to have a magical effect on a person or objects. Incantations don't have to rhyme or be full of fancy words, but they need to be spoken like you mean them, which is why getting good at affirmations can help you enhance your magical abilities.

HOW TO CHOOSE AND ACTIVATE YOUR CRYSTALS

Crystals aren't just pretty chunks of stones that beautify an altar (though they do that too!). Crystals are minerals from under the ground that can absorb and direct energy, and they can be used for a variety of magical and healing purposes. From getting rid of bad vibes to helping you cast spells, crystals are a witch's best friend.

Types of crystals

There are an abundance of crystals out there to choose from and use. Here are some of the most popular.

- **Amethyst** is a purple stone that can protect from negative energy and help relieve stress and strain. It is also said to boost magical powers and help make people more aware of their surroundings

- **Clear quartz**, as its name suggests, is all about clarity. It clears the mind, body and spirit of any clutter and helps with concentration and memory

- **Rose quartz** is a pinkish crystal that is said to enhance all types of love, whether that be self-love, love for others or unconditional love

- **Black tourmaline** is said to be able to soak up negative vibes and get rid of toxicity. It can also make you feel more grounded when life gets a bit much

- **Citrine** is bright yellow and its cleansing properties can help when you're feeling stuck to restore good vibes and confidence

- **Jade** is green and brings good luck in money and relationships. It is said to help improve a sense of balance, stability, peace and wisdom

- **Obsidian** is a powerful volcanic crystal used for protection and to shield you against negativity

Charging crystals

Before you can use crystals in spells, you need to activate or 'charge' them with an intention. To do this, be as clear as possible about what you need and want to achieve in your spell. Then, hold the crystal you want to charge in one hand. Push into the crystal with your other hand as you think deeply about what you want, anything from soothing a headache to finding a friend. Visualise the outcome of your intention as though it's already happened. How will you feel when your wish comes true? The more energy and enthusiasm you can put into this, the stronger the crystal's power will be. You charge the crystal by filling it with the energy you feel during your visualisation. Once it's charged, it's ready to use.

Using crystals

Once your crystal is charged with your intention and desire, you can begin to use it. You can use crystals in a lot of different ways. You can carry them with you so you can focus on the crystal's energy and what you want it to do at any time. You can also wear crystals in jewellery. This works well because the crystal is in constant contact with your skin, making you more conscious of its energy. You can add crystals to your bath to help cleanse and soothe your energy, mind and body. One way to use a crystal in spell casting is to lay it on top of a sheet of paper on which you've written an intention to give that wish the energy it needs to come to life.

Cleansing crystals of negative energy

Cleansing your crystals is another process you can't skip! It is a vital process if you want to be able to harness their full potential. You should even cleanse any new crystals you buy or are gifted, to get rid of any negative energy they hold. You should also cleanse crystals you use regularly to refresh them and remove any negative energy they've absorbed. Methods of cleansing crystals include placing them in a bowl of salt water, smudging them with sage smoke or leaving them in direct sun or moonlight.

DRESSING THE CANDLE/MAKING AN ANOINTING OIL

Candles are a staple item in any witch's box of tricks. Candles can be used to increase and release energy, and they can be used in rituals and spells. Candle flames are associated with fire (obviously!) and fire represents transformation. Fire changes everything it touches and candles help you to tap into that transformational energy when you're doing magic to spark and speed up changes in your life.

Candle colours

Colour symbolism is a key factor in the candle you should choose for different spells. Different colours store different types of energy, and it's those different forms of energy you want to tap into when you burn a candle. Note that as well as choosing coloured candles for their individual properties, you can also combine colours. So, if you're feeling upset after an argument with a loved one, you could burn a pink and a blue candle. The blue helps you heal the hurt and the pink restores your loving connection.

Dressing a candle

Just as you need to charge a crystal to be able to use it in a magic spell or setting, you also need to charge a candle to instil it with magical intent. This is known as 'dressing' a candle. Dressing a candle charges it with energy and intention. Before doing this, set aside some time when you won't be disturbed and find a quiet place, such as your altar, to do it. The more focused you can be, the stronger the intentions with which you will charge your candles.

First, research what kind of oils will support your spell.

Then, set your intention and be very clear about what you want to achieve. Don't simply say, 'I want a job'; say something along the lines of, 'I will get a new job in theatre by the end of the year and I will be a success at it'.

Next, cleanse your candle. Cleansing helps remove any negative energy the candle has picked up. To do this you can wave sage or incense smoke over your candle with a feather or by hand, bury it in sea salt for 24 hours or leave it outside overnight when there is a full moon.

To dress your candle, cover it in an essential oil that is aligned with your intention. If you want to bring something new into your life, rub the oil from the top to the middle, then from the bottom to the middle. If you want to let go of something or send something away, rub oil from the middle outwards to the top and bottom.

To increase your magic, make sure you clearly state your intention as you rub the candle with oil, focusing on your goal and mentally pouring that vision into the candle.

Make your own dressing oil

Here is a recipe for some basic dressing oil for your candles. You need a 150 ml jar with a lid, some carrier oil such as coconut, jojoba, apricot kernel, sweet almond, olive, grapeseed or sunflower oil, and your essential oils or herbs. The idea of using a carrier oil is that essential oils are expensive, so mixing just a few drops into some cheaper carrier oil makes it go further.

To make the dressing oil, clean the jar inside and out, measure out your essential oils as you like, or as per the spell recipe. In general, add 50 ml of the carrier oil, then the essential oils and/or herbs, and then a second 50 ml measurement of carrier oil. Put the lid on the jar and shake vigorously. Keep this in a cool, dark place and shake the jar twice a day to mix the ingredients. If the dressing oil doesn't feel strong enough, add a few more drops of each essential oil.

BUILDING YOUR GRIMOIRE

Hocus-pocus – time to focus! And what better way to collect your witchy magical thoughts, recipes and plans together than in a grimoire? A grimoire is a fancy name for a witch's book. Simply put, a grimoire is a reference created by witches to organise everything they've learnt. Grimoires can be full of spells, information on the different branches of witchcraft (such as tarot, crystals, spellwork etc.) and witchy tips and tricks.

The joy of a grimoire

Most modern witches learn their craft from a lot of different sources, from any number of websites, blogs and books on the subject, and from fellow witches. They read and learn some aspects of the craft that suit them, and some that don't. No two witches are the same. Most witches work by trial and error, or instinct, taking on the spells or rituals that work for or ring true to them, and ignoring or dropping the parts that don't gel. A grimoire is a great place to store the information, tools, tips and tricks that you want to use in your practices for future reference. That way, whenever you forget the meaning of a crystal or colour or need a spell to conjure up some courage, you can open your grimoire and find exactly what you need.

Choose your grimoire

The first thing to do is decide what sort of grimoire you want to create. A grimoire can be made in many different ways. Some witches choose giant, ancient-looking books with parchment style paper to use as their grimoires. More modern-minded witches type up their notes and keep them in a document file. You can buy special journals to use as grimoires, use ring binders or even scrapbooks. Scrapbooks work well as you can add photos or articles taken from magazines or online. Some witches like simple lined paper with colour coded sheets to help them organise their thoughts. Many witches like to handwrite their entries in a sketchbook, so they can add sketches and make their calligraphy big and flamboyant.

Get organised

You might admit to being quite unorganised in daily life, but it really helps to get your grimoire in order, whatever format you choose for your witchy handbook. If it's messy and your spells are scattered between the pages, how will you find the right information when you urgently need it? One safe choice is a ring binder style grimoire, where you have the option to rearrange and add pages as you go.

Decide how to categorise the information in your grimoire. Will you group the spells alphabetically by subject? For example, H for 'healing spells' would come before L for 'love spells'. Will you have sections on 'candle spells', 'jar spells', and 'affirmation spells'? It really helps to include an index at the end of the book and to make sure you leave lots of blank pages between categories so that you don't run out of space as you add more and more information to your grimoire over time.

Have fun with it

Get creative and make your grimoire a pleasure to see and hold. It's a book all about rituals and magic, so it should look spellbinding and mystical to you as well! There are so many ways to decorate a grimoire. You could press flowers and herbs between its pages, add stamps, photographs, stickers or other embellishments. You could use border scissors to cut the edges of the pages into different shapes. Go to town on the cover. If you're big on crystals, you could even draw or attach smaller gems on the cover of your grimoire.

INTRODUCTION TO SPELLS AND INCANTATIONS

Have you ever made a wish while blowing out your birthday candles or knocked on wood for good luck? Then you, like most of us, have already used a ritual of some kind to try to make your hopes and dreams come true. A spell is basically just a special way of asking for something you want.

Spells can help you in almost any way you want. They can help you ease the pain of a broken heart or cut negative energy from your life. They can help you find peace and happiness and improve your relationships with friends and family. They can protect you from problem people and make your personal space feel safer. They can help you get a new job, a pay rise, enjoy success in a project or exam, or even inject some passion into your love life. Casting spells is fun and empowering. Anybody can cast simple spells. You just need an open mind and a willingness to experiment, and soon enough you will harness your inner power and witchy wonderfulness to transform your world!

How spells work

Spell casting is a powerful way of focusing an intention to manifest a goal. They can help us become more focused and determined to get what we want. Most spells consist of three steps: creating an intention, invoking it through a ritual, and putting that intention into action. So, for example, you might decide you want to date that person you have a crush on. That's your intention. You invoke your intention through a ritual like a love spell. This spell helps you put your intention into action, like finally opening up that dating app or finding the courage to text your crush.

Spells are powerful manifestations. When we go through the process of gathering ingredients, creating a sacred space and performing spells, we feed the intention behind our wishes. This makes them stronger. Such spell casting might not look as dramatic and explosive as what we see in films, but they're still quietly powerful!

Do it like you mean it!

Casting a spell is a great way to focus on what you want in life and set your intentions towards your goals, and some say the most important part of any spell *is* your intention. Your intention is critical to casting spells. Magic spells are used to increase the power of your mind and your control over that power. So, while spell casting is and should be fun to do, you also need to commit to it. Spells will only work if they're backed up with some real conviction and commitment.

Spell casting can take many forms, from candle burning, crystal gazing, incantations, rituals and bathing. Get ready to dive into a variety of spells to begin your journey as a fledgling witch, but feel free to expand or adjust these spells as you see fit. There's no correct or incorrect way to make magic, and that's what makes it so special. You can choose to follow a spell to the letter, or use it as inspiration to create your own power-summoning ceremony.

SPELLS FOR HEALTH AND WELLNESS

Sweaty workouts, crossfit crazes, probiotics and kombucha... there's a bewildering array of options of supplements, routines and wonder foods out there to help you stay fit and healthy. The choices we make with regard to our diet and fitness obviously impact on how well we feel. What if magic is the missing ingredient in your day-to-day regime? Learning to perform magic spells is a way of becoming empowered and taking back control of your life and destiny. When it comes to health and wellness, using sorcery for protection and curing ailments is all about being the healer of oneself.

Making magic

Magic spells for health and wellness take a variety of forms. One easy thing we can all do is be mindful about reserving a little time each day to focus on our mental and physical health. The intentions and manifestations associated with magic spells are a great way to help you tap into that energy. Casting spells can help you take control of your health and wellness with a new glow of positivity, and they are a great way to replace lethargy with a fresh flow of enthusiasm. Herbs, spices and other botanicals used in witchcraft can help too. Plants used as incense, in the form of oils, or eaten as food also help us absorb their magical qualities. Our immune system is our body's first line of defence and protects us from both negative energy and unwanted bugs and germs, and one way to boost that immune system is with healing and protective medicinal herbs – ideal magic for health and wellness.

Take care of yourself

Spells help maintain health and wellness but like any magic, they have to be backed up with real-world action. Spells and affirmations can also help empower you to follow a path of self-care and remain a well witch for good. Here are a few ideas.

- Eating well benefits your appearance, your fitness and your state of mind. Just small improvements, like drinking more water and eating more fresh fruit and vegetables will all contribute to your inner and outer glow.

- Rest and relaxation matter. Aim to get seven hours of sleep and make time to switch off from daily stresses and strains and enjoy yourself with friends and family. This will help recharge those batteries and boost your wellbeing.

- Bad habits drag us down. It goes without saying, but too many sugary cakes or salty chips will weigh you down, physically *and* spiritually. Also, try to avoid indulging in too much alcohol and ditch those cigarettes. The only things we recommend lighting up are your candles or your incense!

- Sweat it out! Exercise has countless benefits and by simply making the conscious choice to move a little more each day, your health, skin, posture and physique will all improve.

- Be mindful. For total wellness, take care of what you allow into your head. Angry online arguments or endless social media envy are recipes for misery and low self-esteem. Give yourself some head space and take as much care of your mind as you do your body.

GOOD TO KNOW

Before you dive into the world of self-healing, a word of caution. Some of the spells you'll find in this section are designed to help with ailments such as headaches or colds. They include herbal and natural remedies that can have big health and wellness benefits, but remember to seek medical advice for any progressive and/or prolonged ailments. If you continue to feel unwell or you have any signs of a worsening condition, don't delay – book a doctor's appointment as soon as you can. Perhaps take a charm or crystal along with you for luck and protection?

Good Health Spell Jar

Spell jars are sometimes called 'witches' bottles' and they are handy tools that you can use to perform lots of different kinds of spells. A spell jar is like a physical representation of a spell. Making a spell jar with the right mix of ingredients can help you use your power to amp up the energy behind your intentions. This spell jar is a great remedy to make for yourself when you need a pick-me-up or as a preventative measure to keep you healthy and well.

You will need:

- A glass jar with lid
- Rosemary
- Calendula
- Sage
- A daisy

- Black salt
- Small crystals for protection and luck, such as amethyst, rose quartz or black obsidian
- A blue candle

1. Pick a quiet time and space, such as your altar, where you can be calm and undisturbed. You want an ample opportunity to really enjoy making your jar, to infuse it with good energy.

2. Gather together all your ingredients and place them in front of you. You don't want to interrupt the spell by having to run off to the kitchen to fetch something you've forgotten halfway through!

3. Put the ingredients in the jar, one by one, arranging them in a way that looks pleasing to you.

4. As you put the ingredients carefully into the jar, repeat an affirmation of your choice about your health. You could say something like: "I am fit and I am healthy", or "My body has all it needs to be well".

5. Light your candle, screw the lid on the jar and seal it using some of the molten candle wax. It's important to seal a spell jar with candle wax in a colour that represents your intention. Here you are using a blue candle for healing, health and calmness. Repeat your intention as you seal your spell jar with the wax.

6. Put your finished spell jar somewhere you can see it and experience its energy often, like a bedside table.

Cure a Cold Spell

Feeling run down, sick of a runny nose or coping with irritating aches and pains? This self-healing spell might help! It can also ease the pain of a range of emotional troubles, from suppressed anger to a broken heart. A healthy diet and appropriate exercise will strengthen your constitution.

You will need:

- Eucalyptus oil
- Lavender oil
- An oil burner
- Somewhere comfortable to sit or lie down

1. Put one drop of eucalyptus oil and two drops of lavender oil into the oil burner and light it. Eucalyptus oil has a strong, refreshing evergreen scent and can soothe coughs, colds and infections. Lavender is used to calm and heal the mind and body.

2. While the oils on the burner are warming up, find yourself a comfortable place to sit near to the oil burner so you can breathe in its scents. You might like to sit on a sofa or bed so you can lie down later. Take some long, deep breaths in and out, focusing on feeling your breath flow in and out of your body.

3. Now lie down and close your eyes. Keep breathing deeply and inhaling the spellbinding scents of the essential oils.

4. Take a moment to visualise a clockwise spiral of golden light in front of you. Then imagine another golden spiral moving anti-clockwise beside it. Pull the spirals towards you and towards each other and into your body. To witches, the spiral is symbolic of the journey of life, of growth, change and progress. Try to feel positive energy moving through you, feeding you with its healing powers.

Imagining the spirals may not come easily to you at first, but don't give up. It's really worth persevering and even the act of concentration as you try to do this will help you to feel more relaxed and grounded, while the healing powers of the essential oils also take effect.

A Fire Cider Spell

Herbs have been long used in myths and throughout history to ward off all kinds of ill-health, bad energies and danger – garlic is a key vampire deterrent! This spell helps you to harness the healing powers of herbs and spices. Many of the herbs in your witch's pantry contain antimicrobial and antiviral properties that will help to protect you from illness, as well as negative energy. Infusing this immune-boosting health tonic with a magical intention helps to release its power.

You will need:

- A glass jar with lid
- Fresh herbs and vegetables, such as chillies, oregano, sage, thyme, garlic, horseradish, onions, ginger and turmeric
- Apple cider vinegar
- Honey (optional)

1. First, chop your vegetables and herbs into pieces. Don't be afraid to play around with the ingredients at this point. You can add different herbs and vegetables to your liking, but aim for those known for their immune-boosting qualities.

2. Next, pack them into a clean jar and pour over enough apple cider vinegar to ensure the vegetables and herbs are fully immersed.

3. Hold your hands over the jar and repeat an affirmation such as "I will feel well, I will feel well".

4. Store this new mixture in a cool dark place for 2-4 weeks.

5. Strain your mixture of the pickled vegetables and dispose of them.

6. Take a shot of your Fire Cider potion regularly, especially during the cold and flu season or if you have been directly exposed to someone who is sick. It's an amazing balance of spicy, sour, sweet, sharp and herbal flavours, but if it's not to your liking you can add a spoonful of honey to sweeten it. Instead of drinking a shot of it as it is, you can also dilute your Fire Cider potion with warm water, juice or apple cider if that helps it go down.

Poppet Magic Healing Spell

Poppet magic uses a doll to represent the person on whom the healing magic is to be focused. Poppets are simple to make and it's a fun, creative and caring spell to cast. Poppets can be made of anything you have to hand, from clay to sticks or even aluminium foil. In this spell, you'll make one from fabric.

You will need:

- Two pieces of fabric, around 12 cm x 12 cm
- Glue or a needle and thread
- Chalk
- A pair of scissors
- Coloured pens or thread for decoration
- Camomile flowers
- Vervain or lavender
- A black marker or some bandages
- Salt

1. Lay two pieces of fabric on top of each other. Using the chalk, draw an outline of a simple body, a bit like a gingerbread man.

2. Cut out the pieces and stitch or glue them together around the edges, leaving an opening of an inch or two wide down one side.

3. Stitch or draw a face on your poppet. Get as creative as you like!

4. Use the hole you've left in the seam to add something inside the doll that represents you or the person you want to heal, such as a lock of hair or a scrap of fabric from their clothes.

5. Add the healing herbs and flowers to the inside as well and stitch or glue the opening closed.

6. Now the doll is complete, to intensify the healing powers of the herbs inside, you can draw a black circle on the poppet where the ailment is concentrated, or bandage the part that is hurt (for example, a broken leg).

7. Place the poppet on your altar, close your eyes and visualise yourself or the sick person being in vibrant health.

8. Once the recipient of the spell is better, sprinkle salt on the poppet to separate it from the energy of the person it represented, and dispose of it.

Self–healing Spell

Wellness is about more than your physical health. Wellness means feeling good in your heart and mind too. Stress and emotional pain can start to affect our physical wellbeing. So, this self-healing spell is designed to tackle emotional pain. This can mean anything from a broken heart, anxiety, stress or any other emotional strain that is holding you back from wellness.

You will need:

- Pink cotton fabric square, around 12 cm x 12 cm
- Pink ribbon
- Willow leaf
- Spearmint
- Cinnamon
- Lavender
- Lemon balm
- Quartz crystal

1. Hold the quartz in your hands, close to your heart. Quartz is a great healing stone. You can use it to bring yourself back into balance or to amplify any positive intentions.

2. As you hold the quartz, let your heartache or worries rise to the surface. Cry if you need to. Try to let the pain out and let the quartz crystal absorb some of that negative, damaging energy.

3. Lie your pink fabric square on your altar. Pink is a good colour choice for spiritual and emotional healing.

4. Place the willow leaf in the centre of the fabric. Willow helps to overcome sadness and has healing properties.

5. Lay the quartz on the leaf and then sprinkle the herbs one by one in a circle around the crystal. These herbs help with protection, healing, mental clarity and serenity.

6. As you sprinkle the herbs, state your intentions, either out loud or in your head. For example: "I am whole, I am well".

7. Gently fold the corners of the fabric over to wrap up the herbs, taking care not to spill any. Then you can roll the parcel into a scroll shape. Tie your fabric scroll up with the pink ribbon.

8. Sleep with this parcel under your pillow.

9. When you feel better, you can dispose of the spell. You can scatter the herbs outside, cleanse the quartz for reuse and wash and reuse the fabric square and ribbon if you feel you might need to cast the spell again.

Self–care Bath Spell

Self-care is vital on the path to wellness. Self-care is about valuing yourself and making time to nurture yourself. A beautiful, restful self-care bath not only soothes your muscles but also renews your spirit. The key to making this ritual work is to free up some uninterrupted time.

You will need:

- Bath salts
- Rose petals
- Your favourite fragrance
- Candles: pink is ideal to promote a bit of self-love, and blue helps with emotional healing
- Candleholders (optional)

1. Light the candles and place them around your bathtub. Make sure they're all in candleholders or on a flat, safe surface.

2. As you fill the bathtub with warm water, remind yourself of your intention to love and value yourself.

3. Add your bath salts and rose petals to the water and get into the tub. Salts are perfect for absorbing and unburdening you of any negative energy, and rose petals help you to connect to a romantic atmosphere.

4. As you sink into the warm embrace of the bathwater, visualise yourself connecting with loving energy. Think about everything that you like about yourself and be grateful for all the wonderful things your amazing body allows you to do.

5. After your bath, drain the tub and blow out the candles. (Blowing candles out is a common method of finishing a spell.)

6. Put on your favourite perfume, cologne or body lotion. Take time to massage the scented cream or liquid into your skin.

7. Sit and think again about your intention to practise more self-love. Enjoy how it feels to pamper and love yourself!

Write Your Own Future Spell

A planning and projecting journal is a good way to magically manifest yourself into a more mindful, magnificent future version of you. When you keep a journal for your life plans, you focus on the positive changes you want to bring to your life to improve your health and wellness. To work, these journals rely on the magical powers of manifestation, gratitude and being open to change.

You will need:

- A blank book
- A candle
- Frankincense or cinnamon incense
- A pen

1. Take a few long, deep breaths to centre yourself. Light a candle and burn incense to add a little magic to your space. Cinnamon or frankincense incense sticks are ideal here, as they can enhance your concentration and creative mind.

2. Before you start your journal, take some time to reflect on what you would like to change about your health and wellness.

3. Now, take a few moments to focus on the future version of yourself that you want to become. How do you want to feel, how do you want to act, and what would you like to be doing in the future?

4. Write a future date on a page of your journal and below it write down your intentions. Visualise yourself in that future role.

5. Now write two or three things that you can do to achieve those intentions. Don't make this list impossibly daunting and long. Start with a couple of attainable improvements that you want to make, like eating more vegetables or exercising for half an hour a day.

6. While rereading your intentions, state a strong, positive affirmation to solidify those commitments, to build your confidence and belief that you can achieve your goals. Something like: "I can achieve anything I set my mind to".

You can write in your journal every day or week, or return to it as often as you need to in order to keep your goals fresh in your mind.

Healing Spell for Another

Charging a candle is all about instilling it with magical intentions. In this spell, you can charge a candle with the intention of helping a sick friend or loved one. Ritual candles are chosen for their colour correspondences and are carved, dressed or anointed with special oils chosen for their particular energy.

You will need:

- A white candle
- A toothpick
- Cinnamon oil
- Eucalyptus oil
- Mint oil
- A photo of the person you want to perform the healing spell for
- A large fireproof tray or plate

1. First, carve the name of the person who is in need of help into the candle with the toothpick. White candles are ideal for new beginnings and fresh starts.

2. Next, you should dress the candle with a few drops of the essential oils. All three of the oils used here provide powerful healing energies, and cinnamon will boost the magical power of your spell. As you anoint the candle with the oils, visualise healing energy in the form of white light flowing from your hands and into the candle.

3. Place the photo in the centre of the fireproof tray or plate and sit the candle on top of the photo. (If you don't have a photo, write their name onto a piece of paper instead.)

4. Light the candle and as it burns down, focus on the person in the photograph and think about them being filled with energy and glowing with wellness. You are willing them to be well again. If there is a particular type of healing that the person needs, direct the healing energy to that ailment. So, if they're suffering from a headache or migraine, imagine focusing positive healing energy towards their head. The stronger and longer you can focus, the more likely your spell is to work.

5. Continue to focus and recite for as long as you like, then blow out the candle.

Water Wellness Spell

The key to this spell's success lies in the strength of your desire for it to work and your self-belief. Again, as with all other spells, the more specific you are with your intention, the more specific the results will be.

Everybody has hang-ups, but you shouldn't let them damage your sense of self-worth. This is a confidence-boosting spell for the times we feel unhappy in ourselves.

You will need:

- A bunch of brightly coloured flowers
- A cushion
- A mirror
- A clear glass filled with water

1. Find a time and space when you can do this spell undisturbed.
2. Arrange the flowers in a circle on the floor, big enough for you to sit in.
3. Place the cushion in the centre and the glass of water beside it.
4. Stand or prop the mirror opposite the cushion so that you can look into it when you are sitting down.
5. Sit on the cushion and hold the glass of water between your hands.
6. Look yourself in the eyes in the mirror and focus on putting all of your positive and healing energy into the water.
7. Say your intention out loud or in your head. For example, if you need help with headaches, you could say, "My headache is gone and my head is clear", or if you want to feel a boost in your self-esteem, you could repeat, "I am whole, I am confident, I am proud to be me".
8. Feel the energy from your affirmations entering the water in your glass. Look at the confident, self-assured and determined person in the mirror.
9. Once you feel as though you have put all the necessary energy into the water, you can drink it. Make sure you drink the glass of water within an hour of your casting.

Sleep Spell Jar

A good night's sleep possesses a magic all of its own. We all know the difference between waking up after a solid seven hour snooze and dragging yourself from your bed after a restless night of tossing and turning. Sleep plays a vital role in your physical and mental wellbeing and a lack of it can increase your chances of getting ill. There are a number of things you can do to improve your night-time slumber. Getting into a regular night-time routine is great self-care practice: have a bath, go to bed at a reasonable time (preferably the same day you woke up!) and turn off your phone or tablet an hour before lights out. Making a sleep spell jar can also help you conquer insomnia, bad dreams or regularly waking in the middle of the night.

You will need:

- A glass jar with lid
- Lavender
- Camomile
- Passionflower
- Valerian
- Lemon balm
- An amethyst crystal
- A white candle

1. First, put on some soothing, peaceful music to get you in a restful mood while you make this spell jar. A recording of ocean waves or rain pattering would be ideal.

2. Light the candle. The colour white can help to protect you from negative forces.

3. Place all your ingredients in your jar, one by one. Add the amethyst crystal last. Amethyst will help you to drift into a deep sleep, reduce the risk of nightmares and ease the effects of insomnia.

4. As you add the objects to the jar, think about what your intentions are for your sleep and how you need this spell jar to help you.

5. When the jar is filled, screw on the lid and seal it with molten candle wax.

6. Place your sleep spell jar beside your bed, where it can use its powers to give you a good night's rest. Gaze at it as you drift into the land of nod and focus on the benefits it will bring.

SPELLS FOR PEACE AND HAPPINESS

Everything is energy. When you spend a day with someone who is negative, you can absorb some of that energy and return home feeling anxious and drained. When you spend a day with a bunch of fun, inspiring and loving people, you walk away feeling refreshed and uplifted, like you can be and achieve anything because you've absorbed some of their positive energy. In this section, you'll find spells you can call upon to help you rid your life of negative energy, creating space for positive vibes that will help you to find peace and happiness.

Face your demons

Most of us are generally optimistic and have a 'glass half full' attitude to life. We try to wake up and get out of bed with a positive frame of mind and feel grateful for the good things in our lives. However, there are lots of things that can bring us down. Bad news stories can make you feel depressed and helpless. An argument with a friend can leave you feeling emotionally bruised and fed up. Being rejected from a job or by a crush can knock your confidence and self-esteem. Or, maybe you have too much to do and not enough time to do it in? Think about what it is that's weighing you down. Are there several problems holding you back from finding happiness? Whatever they are, imagine what your life would be like without those worries. It's time to take action to tackle some of these demons. And one way to do that is with affirmations and spells.

Be the change

Magic spells and affirmations can go a long way in helping you find peace and happiness, but using this kind of witchcraft won't always prevent you from feeling pain or sadness in the future. So alongside spell casting and rituals, save some of your amazing energy to stay focused on managing your own thoughts, feelings and behaviours. This way, you can cope with hurdles you meet along the way and leap over them more easily so they don't form a barrier blocking your joy and serenity.

Here are several things we can all do to help us throw open the door to contentment and peace.

- Avoid toxic people. The people you socialise with affect the way you think, feel, and behave. Being around people who lie, gossip, bully or cheat will eventually take a toll on your wellbeing, so reduce contact with them or cut them off.

- You can't always prevent bad things from happening, but you can stop blaming yourself or bad luck. Bad stuff happens to everyone. It's how you *deal* with it that counts.

- Believing you should be happy all the time is not realistic or attainable! Instant gratification will never satisfy us in the long run. Sometimes working hard, however difficult it may be, eventually brings happiness when you reach long-term goals.

- Take a chance. Getting out of your comfort zone might be difficult sometimes, but being temporarily uncomfortable is a small price to pay for the happiness and better life those new experiences can give you!

- Be yourself. Don't waste your life trying to make everyone like you. A person who is liked by everyone on the planet must be some sort of chameleon! Learn to be comfortable in your own skin and know your own worth.

The following spells for peace and happiness can help you address some causes of stress and anxiety in your life. They can help you become a fulfilled, healthy and happy you. They can help you create a harmonious home environment and ward off work worries with stress-relieving spells. You will use crystals for calm and healing and essential oils to conjure up enchantments and rituals for relaxation and letting go. You'll learn how to make soothing teas, blessed brews and potions to help you find your joy.

A Mind–Cleansing Bath

If you're feeling stressed, confused or upset, it's sometimes hard to see how you'll rediscover those old feelings of peace and happiness. Making time for a long and relaxing spiritual bath can help you to replace those negative feelings with tranquility and clarity. First, you will mix a bath potion with ingredients imbued with powers to relieve anxiety and give a sense of calm.

You will need:

- A glass jar
- 1 cup Epsom salts
- 1/2 cup coarse Himalayan pink salt
- Lavender oil
- Rosemary oil
- Geranium oil
- Rose oil

1. First, add the salts to the jar.

2. Then, measure out a total of 20 drops of essential oil. This should be made up of eight drops of lavender oil, six drops of rosemary oil, three drops of geranium oil and three drops of rose oil. Add these to the jar.

3. Next, infuse your potion with positivity. To do this, simply hold your hands over the open jar of salts and oils and visualise love and positivity flowing from your heart, down your arms, through your hands and fingers and into the potion.

4. Run yourself a hot bath and pour the potion into the bath water. As you do so, focus your mind and energy on what the potion will help you to achieve. You could repeat these or similar words: "With this potion I infuse the water with tranquility and clarity, peace and happiness".

5. Get into the bath and lie there quietly, with your eyes closed, absorbing the potion's power and breathing in its spellbinding scents.

6. Stay there as long as you like, or until the bathwater gets cold!

Happiness Spell Jar

Spell jars are a place to gather the thoughts and desires you want to put into your intended spell. When it comes to a happiness jar, it's best to get really specific about what items you choose that remind you of the kind of happiness you seek. Choose objects that really spark joy in you. The list below gives some ideas of things you could add to your jar, but be creative and find your own, if you prefer.

You will need:

- A glass jar with lid
- A photo of you from a day when you felt really happy
- A small piece of fabric from an old favourite top
- A crystal or two to bring happiness, such as citrine or peridot
- Wildflower petals
- Uplifting incense, such as ylang-ylang or patchouli
- A piece of paper
- A pen
- A yellow candle

1. First, clear your head with a few cleansing breaths or some meditation. Do whatever suits you to get into a positive headspace. Maybe put some calming music on in the background.

2. Light the incense to help you cleanse your space and feel at peace.

3. Add the photo, fabric, crystals and petals to the jar one at a time, thinking about what each thing represents and how it relates to your intention.

4. Write down your intention on the paper. For example: 'I will feel happy', or 'I am at peace'.

5. Fold this paper three times and place it in the jar.

6. Light the candle and state your intention out loud or in your head. As you do this, visualise how your wish will feel when it comes true.

7. Screw the lid on the jar and seal it with wax from your candle.

8. Place your happiness jar somewhere you'll see it often to remind you of your intention, such as on a bedside table. Looking at it and focusing on the happiness you hope it will bring before sleep and on waking will help to focus its power.

Marigold Good Luck Spell

People who feel happy tend to consider themselves personally lucky. Thinking of yourself as lucky brings about a kind of optimism or gratitude that breeds hope, self-acceptance, connection and other positive experiences. This simple good luck spell harnesses the power and energy of nature to give you good fortune. Try casting this spell on a Sunday to maximise its potential.

You will need:

- 1 candle (choose a colour such as yellow for happiness, white for optimism or green for luck)
- A handful of marigold petals, ideally organic
- Water
- A saucepan
- A teaspoon of white sugar
- A sieve or tea strainer
- A mug

1. Put your saucepan on the stove and turn on the heat. Fill your mug with fresh water from the tap and pour this into the saucepan. When the water is boiling, turn the heat down so the water is gently simmering, and add the marigold petals to the saucepan with the sugar. The sugar symbolises adding a little extra sweet fortune to your brew. Simmer gently for four or more minutes to make your tea infusion.

2. Once it is ready, hold your sieve or strainer over the mug and pour the tea through it, to strain out the marigold petals.

3. Sit your candle next to your mug of marigold tea and light it. Say these words out loud or in your head:

   "As the flame of hope here burns,
   luck and happiness start to turn.
   As I sip this blessed tea,
   serendipity will come to me".

4. Once recited, you can now drink the tea. As you sip, feel the positive energy and good luck vibes entering your body.

Banish Bad Feelings Spell

Is there something holding you back from peace and happiness? Perhaps it is a little bit of lingering anxiety or a memory of someone saying or doing something bad to you? Perhaps it is a feeling of a lack of self-worth that prevents you from feeling joy? You can use this banishing spell to rid yourself of all kinds of bad feelings, thoughts or memories that stand in your way of finding peace and happiness.

You will need:

- A smudge stick
- A stick or wooden spoon (about 15 cm long)
- A piece of cord (about 60 cm long, ideally black)
- A piece of paper
- A pen
- A black candle
- Your favourite black protection crystal

1. Gather all your tools and place the crystal on your altar in front of you. Burn the smudge stick to cleanse your space. Open the windows and doors to your altar room to let out any negative energy.

2. Sit quietly and mindfully and focus your intention on the negative emotion you want to banish from your life. Think about how good you'll feel once this emotion has been expelled from your body and mind.

3. Light the candle and continue to focus on your intentions. Imagine your focus burning as you look at the flame.

4. Write the problem you wish to banish from your life on your paper. Be specific. Wrap this piece of paper around your stick or wooden spoon.

5. Next, slowly begin to wrap the cord round and round the paper and stick/spoon as tightly as you can.

6. As you do this, imagine you are trapping that unwanted energy and it is leaving you. Feel the weight of this negative emotion leave your body. Feel your body relax.

7. When you reach the end of the cord, tuck it into itself so it won't unravel.

8. Place your stick somewhere you can see or find it to remind you of your intention.

Releasing the Pain Spell

Some events or experiences leave us feeling deeply unsafe and often helpless. Feelings of deep emotional pain can result from a single event or be part of an ongoing experience, such as bullying, discrimination or humiliation. This kind of emotional trauma can block the paths that can lead you to peace and happiness in your everyday life. This spell can help to rid you of the fears and anxieties that are holding you back from the happiness you deserve. Perform it in the evening, before going to bed, on a night you have peace and quiet.

You will need:

- A white, yellow or orange candle
- Some cleansing incense, such as clove, cedar or lavender
- Sea salt
- Some aromatherapy oil, such as almond or lavender oil

1. Spend a few minutes cleansing your space. Light the cleansing incense of your choice and let its purifying smoke drift over your space and ingredients.

2. Place the candle in front of you in the centre of your altar or on a flat surface. Sprinkle a circle of purifying and protective sea salt around the candle. Light it.

3. Pour some drops of your chosen aromatherapy oil into your hands and anoint yourself in the same way you would a candle. Ensure the oil is safe for direct skin contact. Rub and massage the oil slowly and rhythmically into whichever part of your body you think feels right.

4. Stare into the candle's flame and, as you do so, recite the below words:

   "Earth below, stars above. Instil the black of night with love.
   The shining Sun will burn away my pain, and I will rise renewed again".

5. Now imagine your emotional pain or anxiety flowing out of your body.

6. Go to bed and focus on your renewed sense of hope and happiness.

Calming Spell Jar

If anxiety and stress is preventing you from enjoying peace and happiness in your life, have a go at making one of these calming spell jars. As always with spell casting, feel free to take or leave what you want from the following ingredients list. You can work with whatever calming ingredients you have in your witch's pantry, if that is more convenient!

You will need:

- A glass jar with lid
- Camomile
- Lavender
- Gardenia
- Bergamot oil

- A bowl
- Water
- Crystals with calming powers, such as amethyst, celestite or malachite
- A purple or light blue candle

1. First, fill the bowl with water and sit it on a windowsill or outdoors (somewhere it can't be disturbed by cats or other animals) so it can bask in the light of a full moon. Let the moon charge your water overnight. Moon water has been used for centuries to help humans embrace and absorb cosmic energy from the full moon.

2. Next, place all your herbs and oils, including the moon water, into your jar. Do this one at a time and as you put each item into the jar, think about the magical properties it contains and how it will help you chase away feelings of anxiety and stress.

3. Light your candle. A light blue candle represents peace, harmony and tranquility. Purple candles are associated with royalty, wealth, ambition, divinity, wisdom, healing, intuition and psychic ability.

4. Now take a few deep breaths and inhale the spellbinding scent emanating from the oils and herbs in your jar. Feel their soothing and calming effect on your mind and body.

5. Next, screw the lid on the jar and seal it with some of the candle wax. Place this jar on a bedside table or your desk to invoke calmness and peace and ward off stress and anxiety.

Smudge Spell for Peace and Happiness

Lavender is a herb that is well known for its calming properties and beautiful, restful scent. Use this herb to bring peace and serenity into your space. You can perform a smudging ritual for protection at any time of the day, so you can use this spell whenever you need it most. Try this spell if you need to clear the air of bad energy, such as after an argument or if you've just had some unwelcome visitors in your home.

You will need:

- Some dried lavender stems
- Twine or string
- A fireproof bowl or abalone shell
- A light blue candle

1. Before you begin your ritual, calm your mind by taking a few deep breaths to centre yourself.

2. Open the window or door to allow any smoke to escape, carrying with it the negative energy that was in your space.

3. Light the candle.

4. Gather the lavender into a bunch with the twine to create a smudge stick, then use the candle flame to light it over the bowl.

5. Think about how you are using all four of the Earth's elements to increase the power of this ritual. Fire is represented by the candle, Earth in the form of the smudging stick, Air in the smoke that is created when the smudging stick has been lit and Water by the bowl or abalone shell you use.

6. As you waft the smoke around yourself and your space, try saying the following out loud or in your head:

   "With this smoke, I expel bad thoughts, emotions and energy from my space".

7. Hold your focused intention throughout the whole process. When you're ready, blow out the candle and let the smudge stick smoulder until it dies out in the bowl.

Drumming Spell

We all know the right kind of music can help us feel more relaxed and settled, but it's a little known fact that drumming can help alleviate stress and anxiety. Most of us associate drums with loud, insistent noise that might do the very opposite of creating serenity. But in many cultures, drums are a sacred tool connecting heaven and Earth, and maintaining the rhythm of life. In this spell, drumming also stimulates acupressure and reflexology points on your hands to produce mood-lifting effects.

You will need:

- Sandalwood incense
- An incense burner
- Brightly coloured ribbons, such as yellow, orange or blue
- A hand drum (for example: a djembe, bongo or conga drum)
- A yellow candle

1. Start by lighting your incense.

2. Then, tie as many ribbons around the drum as you like.

3. Begin tapping on the drum with both hands. There is no right or wrong way to play here, and you're not trying to make a tune. Don't worry about how you sound. Just play. Feel the vibrations from the drum skin quivering through your hands, arms and body. Feel it breaking up the dark, stressful energy around you.

4. As you play on, try to coordinate the drum beats with the beating of your own heart. Let this shared rhythm and connection make you feel joyful and alive.

5. Some people like to close their eyes to help them feel the rhythm more intuitively. With your eyes closed, your senses become more alive and you are more likely to feel the connection between the beating of the drum and the pulsations of your heart. Try to focus only on the drumming and the sensations it gives you.

6. You can repeat this spell whenever you feel down and you should find it gives you a pretty instant boost.

Build a Crystal Grid

A novel way to harness the power of crystals is by building your own crystal grid. A crystal grid is an arrangement of crystals that you create to suit your particular needs and intentions. The idea is that by creating a grid you are magnifying the energetic properties of the crystals, and getting them to work together in a synergistic way. This crystal grid pattern is ideal for stimulating happiness, peace and positivity.

You will need:

- A clear quartz stone
- Four rose quartz stones
- Four citrine stones
- A piece of paper
- A pen
- A compass

1. Find a place that your crystal grid can remain undisturbed. This could be on your altar, or if you are going to use that for other spell casting, find another spot.

2. The first thing to do is determine the reason behind why you're making a grid. Possible intentions could include finding happiness, peace or overcoming anxiety.

3. Next, you need to charge your crystals to align them with your intentions. To do this, simply hold each crystal between your hands while concentrating for a minute or two on the intention you wish to set.

4. Now you will construct your grid. Start by placing the clear quartz crystal in the centre. Clear quartz is used for clarity, healing and spiritual growth.

5. Next, place the rose quartz stones north, south, east and west of the centre stone. Rose quartz is said to boost feelings of self-love.

6. Finally, place the citrine stones between each of the rose stones. Citrines are powerful protection crystals that reduce stress and exhaustion, leaving a feeling of calm flowing throughout the body.

7. Next, write your intention on the paper and place it under the centre stone. Your grid is now finished. Spend a few minutes with it, focusing on its purpose and powers.

Conjure up a Peace Candle

In this simple ritual, you are going to coat ordinary candles with herbs that will help you attain your goals when you light the candle. Thyme is an ideal herb to use here, as it has properties that will help you to purify and cleanse your home and invite in love and peace. Thyme will increase your willpower and give you courage to face down anything that threatens your peace too.

You will need:

- A candle
- A candleholder
- A container or bowl deep enough to stand the candle in
- Some finely chopped dried herbs, such as thyme
- A hairdryer
- A fireproof plate or tray

1. First, focus on your intention and the goal of peace and happiness you want to achieve with this spell.

2. Plug in and turn on the hairdryer and run it up and down a 2-4 cm section of the candle so that the hot air slightly melts the outer surface of that part of the candle.

3. Holding the candle by the end, carefully roll it in the herbs. As you roll the candle, the herbs should stick to its molten surface.

4. Once that section is coated, then do another section of the candle, and so on until the candle is completely coated. (You may have to pause now and then to let the candle cool and solidify, to avoid it getting too sticky to handle.)

5. Once the candle is fully covered in the herbs, hover the hairdryer over the entire candle again so that the wax really soaks in.

6. Sit the candle in a holder over a fireproof plate or tray. Light the candle.

7. Breathe in its scent and focus on its flame as you dwell on your intentions.

SPELLS FOR FRIENDS AND FAMILY

Relationships are a huge part of our lives. We can't live without them. They can be challenging, of course, but in the long run they are one of the most important things in life. Building healthy relationships with friends, family and partners is good for you. When relationships are working well, your mood, mental health and wellbeing are all positively impacted. When relationships fracture, it can impact on every aspect of your life.

The relationship rollercoaster

Relationships with friends and family are likely to go through testing times and there will always be ups and downs. It's like being on a relationship rollercoaster. One minute you're laughing and the next you could be screaming! Sometimes people you care about will let you down and sometimes you'll let them down. It can feel like you do nothing but argue with a sibling or find it impossible to talk to a parent. What if a friend becomes a negative force in your life and starts to drag you down? Or perhaps a relationship you care about is breaking down because of neglect? Spells can help.

Making magic happen

Casting a spell can help you to focus on what you really want out of a relationship. If you're shy and find it hard to make new friends, magic can be a supernatural support. There are rituals you can follow to help you take care of and maintain existing friendships. Some spells are designed to reconnect friends and family who have distanced themselves and forgotten how it feels to have those vital, close connections. If there are people with whom you've had a disagreement or fight and you find yourself in a state of separation or rift, remember these problems can hurt a lot, but they don't have to last forever. Magical intentions can help you heal those wounds. And what if there is someone in your life who bullies or suffocates you with their negative energy? You can use your magical will to help you expel such people from your sphere.

Nurturing relationships

If you don't water that house plant, it'll die. Relationships are similar. They're a living thing. If you don't give them attention, they'll wither away! Magic can help, but it'll only really work if you back it up with some direct action too. Here are some tips for nurturing friends and family to ensure those relationships go on nurturing you too.

- Keep in touch. Call, text, email, write, meet more often.

- Make time. It's important to make time to really talk to or do something fun with friends and family. It's too easy to let the weeks slip by without really making an effort to connect. So, if you haven't had quality time with someone for a while then open your diary and arrange to do so.

- Listen up. When you do get together with a buddy or relative, listen more. Really listen. And try to see things from their perspective.

- Open up. Without suddenly gushing all over your loved ones, try to remember to tell them how much you care about them and what particular things you really appreciate about them once in a while.

- Remember birthdays and important dates. Write them down on a calendar or in your phone! Some people claim they don't care about people remembering their birthday but most of us appreciate even just a text or a phone call. You might not be able to be there in person, but just taking a moment out of your day to consider that loved one helps keep your relationship healthy.

Making Friends Spell

Some people seem to make friends easily, but for others it's a challenge. Do you feel shy or worried about making the first move? Or perhaps you've moved recently or just started at a new college or job. This spell will help you to make and keep new friends.

You will need:

- A blank postcard
- A gold pen
- A bay leaf
- Clear sticky tape
- A 30 cm length of thin, gold ribbon

For maximum effect, do this spell on a Sunday or a Wednesday, or on a new or full moon.

1. The gold pen symbolises success. Use it to write your invocation for new friends. Write it as if it's an ad you might see in a shop window. Write the word WANTED at the top in bold letters and, below that, a description of the kind of friends you're looking for. It should look something like this:

WANTED

Kind and adventurous friends who I can have a laugh with.
Honest, trustworthy and loyal friends who I can confide in and who
like me for who I am.

2. When you're happy with the wording, use the clear tape to stick the bay leaf to the postcard.

3. Gently roll up the postcard and tie the gold ribbon around it, like a scroll.

4. While holding the scroll in your hand, take a few moments to focus on how you will enhance your magic. Remind yourself of all your good and likeable qualities. Think of ways to put yourself out there to talk to and get to know people. Make a personal pact to always be yourself, be persistent and never be too quick to quit.

5. Leave the scroll on your windowsill for 24 hours so that your message will be carried out into the universe. Then put it somewhere safe in your bedroom.

Healing a Rift Spell

Falling out with friends or family is painful. Sometimes things are said in the heat of the moment that feel like they can never be taken back. Sometimes a minor squabble leads to you becoming distanced from each other for a while. This spell can help to heal those rifts. It can work to mend a falling-out between two people or more and to draw them back together.

You will need:

- A thin white candle
- A pink candle
- A toothpick
- Parchment paper
- A pair of scissors (optional)

1. Snap or cut the white candle into evenly sized pieces. The number of pieces you cut should be the same as the number of people you want to bring together. So, if three people are involved, break the candle into three pieces. Leave the wick at the top part of the candle as this symbolises the connection of the people involved.

2. Now you're going to use the toothpick to carve individual names onto the pieces of candle. Each piece should end up with a different name carved into it. As you write the names, imagine positive energy surrounding that person.

3. Place the white candle pieces closely back together on the parchment paper. Say:

   "We're birds of different feathers,
      but, we are better together".

4. Light the pink candle, symbolising love, and drip its molten wax onto the cracks of the divided white candle. The molten wax will join the pieces of the white candle. As it makes the white candle 'whole' again, focus your energy on how it will feel to repair the cracks in your relationship.

5. As the wax hardens, feel your resolve and determination to repair those rifts become firmer and stronger too.

Reconnect with a Friend Spell

Have you and a BFF drifted apart? Has it been forever since you and that old school pal have even spoken to each other? Is there someone you'd like to see and have been meaning to see, but now it's been so long that it feels hard to imagine you'll ever be able to rekindle that friendship? This simple spell will bring back a friendship with a little candle burning ritual. It uses the powers of salt for luck, purification and protection, and cloves, which are often used to help keep good friends close.

You will need:

- 7 cloves
- 1 orange candle
- Sea salt
- A piece of paper
- A pen

1. Light the candle on your altar or table. In this spell we're using an orange candle for balance, memory, sharing and kindness. Lighting the candle symbolises the rekindling of your lost friendship.

2. Write your full name and your friend's full name on the paper.

3. Put the seven cloves and sea salt on top of the names.

4. Close your eyes and focus your mind on a happy memory of a good time you and your friend shared. As you bask in this happy recollection, point your index finger at the names to pass the positive energy from the memory into the paper and repeat these words:

   "With my finger and this refrain
   I ask that we may meet again,
   our strong friendship we'll renew
   and pains of the past we will undo,
   so it shall be".

5. Sit quietly for a few minutes, or as long as it feels right for you, meditating.

6. Then blow out the candle and watch its smoke carrying your request out into the universe.

7. Fold the paper three times and give it to your friend if you feel it would help. Or bury the paper in soil, in the garden or in a plant pot.

Bully Be Gone Spell

Some people we know or we're forced to work or study with are bad news. If someone is pushing you around or bullying you, it needs to stop. Bullying is a serious problem and while spells can help and give you feelings of confidence and power to overcome the bullying, you should also talk to someone who can help stop it. This is a binding spell, designed to bind someone's power, to prevent them from causing harm or pain.

You will need:

- A black candle
- Sea salt
- Black thread
- A pair of scissors
- A piece of paper
- A pen
- A fireproof tray or plate

1. Write the name of the person who is bullying you on the paper and place it on your altar or a table.

2. Light the black candle.

3. Sprinkle a circle of sea salt around the paper, working from the top in a clockwise direction.

4. Cut a piece of black thread and tie it tightly around the paper, crumpling it as you do so. As you do this, repeat these words aloud or in your head:

   "With this spell I bind you [name of bully]. Your insults can no longer hurt me. Your meanness is meaningless. You will bully and intimidate me no more".

5. Repeat this ritual a total of seven times, with a total of seven pieces of black thread.

6. Then blow out the candle. Leave the paper in the ring of salt for 24 hours.

7. Then drop the salt into the bin or flush it down the toilet, and burn the paper on a fireproof plate or tray, or outdoors.

8. Every step of the way during this ritual, try to concentrate your energy on your intentions. Concentrate on thoughts of your happy life without the bullying. Sharpen your determination to take action to get it stopped.

Farewell to a Frenemy Spell

Have you got a friend who is more of a 'frenemy'? Someone who brings out the worst in you, often makes you feel bad about yourself, robs you of your confidence, may try to persuade you to do stuff you know inside is wrong – in short, someone with heavy negative vibes? If you do, then it's time to move on and you can use your witchcraft skills to help you disengage from this toxic person.

You will need:

- Objects that are reminders of the relationship (avoid non-biodegradable items, such as plastic or glass, if you can)
- A box
- A fireproof tray or plate
- Rosemary
- A clove of garlic

1. Collect together a variety of objects that remind you of the frenemy. For example, perhaps a card they sent you, a photo of them, or a ticket you got when you went somewhere together. Or it could simply be something that reminds you of them, like a piece of food they like to eat.

2. Put all of the items into the box.

3. If the objects will burn, take them outdoors, scatter them with some rosemary and set fire to them in the light of the moon on a fireproof plate or tray.

4. If they're biodegradable, bury them with a clove of garlic in a plot at some distance from where you live or work.

5. At this point, if at all possible or practical, let this person know that you wish to discontinue this relationship. You don't have to explain or justify yourself. Avoid giving them a list of their faults and try not to get caught up in a conversation with them. Keep it polite, but firm and simple. Just say something like:

"This isn't working. I no longer want to continue this friendship with you. No hard feelings, but please don't contact me again".

Bickering Brothers and Scrapping Sisters Spell

Friends may come and go, but siblings are forever. Siblings can be really supportive and important. Sometimes siblings clash. If you and your sibling are constantly fighting, then this spell may be for you. But you need to stop squabbling long enough to persuade your sibling to help you cast this spell!

You will need:

- A ball of string
- Two long pieces of white ribbon
- Two long pairs of different coloured ribbons (say, two orange and two blue)
- A bowl of rainwater
- A piece of paper
- A pen
- A white candle in a candleholder

1. First, write what caused your most recent argument on the piece of paper.

2. Then unravel the string and use it to make a circle large enough for you and your sibling to sit in. If you don't have string, you could draw a circle on the floor or sprinkle rainwater in a circle.

3. Place the paper and all the other ingredients you need for the spell in the centre of the circle and then you and your sibling should sit cross-legged within it, opposite each other.

4. Light the white candle. Pick up a piece of white ribbon each. You should both sprinkle rainwater from the bowl on your piece while saying:

   "White is the colour of new dawns; we hope our relationship can now be reborn".

5. Next, you each pick up a piece of coloured ribbon that represents you and sprinkle rainwater on it while saying, "This is my wish, made with all my heart".

6. Now, you each pick up a piece of ribbon that represents the other person and sprinkle rainwater on it while saying, "We are together bound by positivity; we coexist in perfect harmony".

7. You should have three ribbons each now. Plait them together. Then each tie your plaited ribbon around your wrist. This represents your togetherness.

Family Harmony Spell

Is your family fractured by discord and friction? Are you ready to open the door to more harmony and happiness in your family? This spell won't prevent arguments or disagreements from ever happening, but it can bring a renewed sense of family unity into your life.

You will need:

- One pebble (or pieces of moonstone) for each family member
- Sea salt
- Water

1. First, dedicate each pebble in turn to a member of the family. To do this, hold each stone in your hand and say: "You are mother"; "You are father", and so on. You can include as many family members as you like – even grandparents, aunts and uncles.

2. Place the stones on your altar in positions that feel right. For example, family members who don't get along might be farther away from each other. Family members who have a good relationship might go closer together. It becomes a visual representation of where the distances and difficulties lie in the family.

3. Now gradually, stone by stone, move the pebbles into positions of unity, where they should be, such as parents together with children close by, until it looks more like a family unit.

4. Hold your hands over the pebbles and let love flow from your heart and into all of them – even those who represent people with whom you have a difficult relationship!

5. Then, using your hands, gently begin to draw the pebbles even closer together until they all touch.

6. Close your hands over this family of stones and shut your eyes. Think about how important the love of this family is to you.

7. You could repeat this three times a day or draw a circle around the stones on the paper and leave it on the altar for the love to grow.

Stop the Gossip Spell

Words can hurt and unfortunately, once someone has started a false rumour, it can spread quickly. So, what can you do when someone starts spreading mean tidbits of gossip about you? Here is a simple ritual to help you take back your power and stop slander and malicious gossip from affecting you.

You will need:

- Extra virgin olive oil
- A compass
- Five white candles in candleholders
- A toothpick

1. Dress the candles with extra virgin olive oil.

2. Use the toothpick to carve your name into one of the white candles. Place it in its candleholder at the centre of your altar or a table.

3. Use the compass to identify in which direction north lies and then place the other four white candles around the central white candle (representing you) on the altar in the positions of north, south, east and west.

4. Light the central candle and as you do so, say: "Here I stand, I who am being talked about and lied about in malicious gossip. My truth will be known".

5. Light the candle to the west and say: "Truth is behind me, it follows me wherever I may go".

6. Light the candle to the north and say: "Truth is always with me and it will be known".

7. Light the candle to the east and say: "Truth is ahead of me, and will be wherever I go".

8. Light the candle to the south and say: "Truth is the rock and ground upon which I stand".

9. As the candles burn, spend ten minutes in quiet contemplation, imagining white light surrounding you.

10. When you have finished, extinguish the candles.

11. Relight the candles and repeat the ritual every day for three days.

Family Unity Affirmations

Family is an important part of our lives and plays a crucial role in our wellbeing. Sometimes we neglect our families, or families drift apart or get trapped in a cycle of bickering. Affirmations are a great way to switch up the energy in relationship dynamics. Affirmations provide us with a positive mindset and energy. Affirmations can help to shift the balance in any relationship setting because they replace negative thought patterns with more positive ones.

You will need:

- A piece of paper
- A pen
- A mirror

1. First, come up with a set of affirmations that mean something to you and that you can state with conviction. Try some of the examples below.

   "I love my family as I love myself."
   "My parents and siblings are very special to me."
   "I will do my best every day to keep my family happy."
   "I will enjoy family gatherings and make the most of the times we are all together."
   "I will treat my parents with love and respect."

2. You should write down at least two affirmations and start practising them. You can practise by saying them aloud standing in front of the mirror.

3. Repeat this ritual for three to four minutes and try to make time to do it every day.

4. Some people attach their written affirmations to a wall or pinboard so they can see them and read them regularly as constant reminders of their desires.

5. After you've stated your affirmations, take a few moments to focus on the good parts of your family relationships and imagine increasing those moments. Think about when those moments happen, how they feel and what you can do to help make more of them. Think about making time for the different family relationships in your life.

Friendship Spell Jar

Make this friendship spell jar to attract, strengthen and nurture close connections with people. This spell requires a number of ingredients, but each one is chosen to enhance and enrich the wish for meaningful friendships that you're putting out into the universe.

You will need:

- A glass jar with lid
- Sea salt
- Cloves
- A pinch of cinnamon
- Lavender
- A rose quartz crystal
- An amethyst crystal
- Dried dandelion
- A piece of paper
- A pen
- A teaspoon of sugar
- A yellow or white candle

1. On the paper, write down your intentions and wishes for this friendship. Try to be as clear as possible in your words. Say what you hope for in a friend or how you would like an existing friendship to grow and develop.

2. Charge your crystals for this spell. Hold each one in your hand, one by one, and imagine what you wish for and visualise a mind 'film' in which you watch you and your friend being happy.

3. Place both crystals on the piece of paper.

4. Fold the paper three times and then put it and the other ingredients into the friendship spell jar.

5. As you put each ingredient into the jar, think about what it means and how it will help you fulfil your desires.

6. Light your candle, screw the lid on the jar and seal it with molten wax.

7. Place the jar by your bed or somewhere you will be able to look at it and think about what it means.

8. Remember that spell jars work best when followed up with intentions and an open heart that is ready to welcome new friendships or strengthen present friendships.

SPELLS FOR POWER AND PROTECTION

Sometimes the world we live in can feel stressful and dangerous. The news cycles that populate our screens can seem to show endless heartbreaking, violent and chaotic stories and images. Combine that with personal fears that can hang over us like black clouds in our day-to-day lives, and that adds up to a lot of anxiety and worry. Feeling emotionally or physically unsafe is exhausting and can leave you open to absorbing even more negativity. This is where protection spells come in. Whether you are looking to improve your self-confidence, protect yourself from negative energy from outside, or stay safe in a stressful world, protection spells can help.

Protection and power spells are forms of magic you can do to ward off negative energy and strengthen your inner power and self-belief. They can help you to cleanse bad forces from your life and give you confidence that you are safe from danger and negative energy. By working with protection spells, you can protect and defend yourself and your family, reduce stress, banish bad energy, get rid of unpleasant people, repel unhealthy influences and defend your property.

Back it up

Obviously, protection and power shields need to be used wisely. You can't take risks just because you cast a protection spell. Magic spells don't and shouldn't replace other kinds of home security and self-protection. You need to be savvy about staying safe too. Back up your magic with action. You know the drill.

- Avoid risk-taking, such as going on a blind date with someone you've only ever spoken to on an app, spending money you don't have or going over the speed limit.

- Be careful what personal details – including photos – you give out online, by phone or in real life.

- Keep your stuff safe and secure and try to avoid flashing expensive items and jewellery on a night out.

- Listen to your intuition and follow your best judgement. If your friends are making bad decisions, you don't have to follow their lead. Have the confidence to say no if anyone makes you feel uncomfortable about anything.

- Trust your instincts. If you ever feel threatened by a situation or someone, leave. Listen to your body – a fast, pounding heartbeat and churning stomach are signs you feel unsafe.

- Letting someone know where you will be at all times is a smart move. And always make sure you have a fully charged phone before you leave the house. If you are ever faced with a risky situation or get into trouble, your family and friends will know where to find you. Also, never leave home angry because of an unresolved situation and never get behind the wheel of a car when you are upset.

Take back your power

Spells for power and protection help to awaken your inner strength. They help you believe you are not powerless when faced with other people's bad energies or the threat of loss or harm. You have the power to conjure up a forcefield to hold harmful forces at bay by casting a protection spell. Many protection spells work by creating a shield that keeps away evil forces and negative energy. Protection spells also work like banishing spells, which help you get rid of other people's negative energy and stop it from impacting your life or the lives of others you care about.

So, read on to discover spells that will help you feel powerful, banish bad energy, ward off unpleasant people and protect your belongings, your spirit and your space! You're smart and strong and ready to take on the world. Go do it, just use your head and your spells to stay safe out in the big, wide world.

Crystal Jewellery Charms

If you want to relax in the knowledge that you are safe from negative energy all day and every day, one of the best ways to do this is by wearing your protective magic. There are a number of ways in which you can do this. One of the most effective is to infuse your jewellery with magic.

You will need:

- Jewellery that contains crystals or charms that resonate with you and make you feel powerful
- A piece of paper
- A pen

1. Jewellery is a great way to carry your power on you throughout the day. Choose from protective crystals such as obsidian, turquoise or carnelian. Obsidian is a strong psychic protection stone that has powerful properties that will help to shield you against negativity. Turquoise helps to enhance communication and expression and can help you to speak up for yourself when you need to. Carnelian is thought to combat feelings of inadequacy and to increase physical energy. You could wear a combination of different crystals.

2. Find a quiet spot in your home or out in nature where you can sit comfortably.

3. Close your eyes and take some slow, deep breaths to calm your mind and connect with your thoughts.

4. Hold your jewellery in your hand, look at the crystal and think of what it embodies.

5. Before wearing your chosen jewellery, infuse it with a powerful affirmation. For example: "I am gracefully embodying courage as I show up for myself each day with confidence, empowerment and self-love", or "My positive energy is safe from harm because I control it".

6. Repeat your affirmation until you feel it in your heart.

7. Then, write your affirmation on paper and keep it in a spot where you can see and read it every day.

8. Put your piece of jewellery on. When faced with challenges or fears, you should be able to hold or touch your jewellery to connect with the affirmation and the protection it holds.

Smoke Cleansing Spell

Smoke has long been used by people to protect themselves from negative energy to ward off bad intentions. Burning incense is another ancient technique used to cleanse a space. Cleansing energy with a smouldering smudge stick also works effectively. Each plant and herb contains its own magic, so you can choose one that you have to hand or that speaks to you – or one you just like the smell of!

You will need:

- Incense
- Herbs and leaves, such as frankincense, pine, cedar, sage or rosemary
- A candle
- A fireproof tray or plate, or an abalone shell
- Twine or string

1. Gather a bunch of herbs you want to use to cleanse and protect your personal space. Wrap the twine around it to create your smudge stick.

2. Light your candles.

3. Set an intention before setting fire to your smudge stick. For example:

   "As I light this tool, please protect me from any negative energy that tries to hold me back from my path, my joy, my health and my purpose".

4. Then light the smudge stick in the candle flame by holding it at a 45 degree angle and pointing the tip down towards the flame. Allow it to burn for 30 seconds, and then blow it out.

5. Place it on any heatproof surface such as a fireproof tray or an abalone shell.

6. Leave it to smoulder and release smoke for about five minutes.

7. Alternatively, you can walk around your personal space, fanning the smoke all over, whilst focusing your mind on cleansing and clearing any negative energy. If you feel you personally are being affected by negative energy, you can fan the smudge stick around yourself.

8. Your cleansing ritual is now complete.

Protection Spell with Bells

Bells have been used for centuries to ward off evil spirits and cleanse negative energy from an area or space. The word 'bell' comes from Old or Middle English words such as 'bellen' or 'bellan', meaning to roar or make a loud noise (as in to 'bellow'). Make these witch's bells to protect your room and home. As well as having a magical quality, bells of course have a practical purpose. If someone tries to open your door, the bells will ring to alert you to the unannounced visitor.

You will need:

- Small bells with loops to put cord or ribbon through
- Cord or ribbon
- Drawing pins

1. Cut a length of cord or ribbon and use it to tie a set of small bells together. You could add a bow at the top or tie the bell string to a hoop. Get as creative as you like – after all, these bells can double as a decorative ornament in your home. Some people change the ribbons with the seasons or for different festivals.

2. Pin the set of bells to a door or hang them from a window. As you hang them, repeat these words:

   "This space belongs to me. Any negative or threatening energies have no power in this space".

3. Some witches put their protective bells on both the inside and outside of their doors. The great thing about witch's bells is that they are magic hidden in plain sight – there's no need to have to explain their function to those who do not practise witchcraft if you don't want to.

4. Leave your witch's bells to work their magic but remember to take the bells down now and then to cleanse or replace them to keep their magic fully functional and strong.

A Witch's Ladder for Power and Protection

A witch's ladder is a type of 'knot' magic that can be used for a wide variety of purposes. They are commonly made by plaiting or knotting ribbon or cords together while incorporating other materials that represent a particular intention. There are suggestions below for what to include in a witch's ladder for power and protection, but you can use your knowledge of ingredients in your witch's pantry to customise your own if you'd prefer.

You will need:

- Three equal lengths of white, red or black cord or ribbon, at least 1 m long
- Materials to weave into the cords (such as feathers, herbs, beads, crystals or charms)
- Metal ring (optional)

1. Tie all three cords together at one end, or you can tie them to a metal ring.

2. Braid the cords together and weave in feathers and other items as you go along.

3. You should incorporate nine knots into your ladder. Some people like to tie a knot where they weave in a charm or other item to ensure it stays firmly anchored.

4. As you make the ladder, you imbue it with magical energy by keeping your goal firmly fixed in your mind and visualising your intentions.

5. When the ladder is almost finished, recite this simple spell while touching each one of the eight knots you have created, then tie the ninth knot as you say the last line.
   "By knot of one, the spell's begun.
   By knot of two, the magic comes true.
   By knot of three, so it shall be.
   By knot of four, this power is stored.
   By knot of five, my will shall drive.
   By knot of six, the spell I fix.
   By knot of seven, the future I leaven.
   By knot of eight, my will be fate.
   By knot of nine, what is done is mine."

6. Now you can hang the ladder on a door, a curtain rail or above your bed or desk to give you the power and protection you seek.

Freezing Spell

Is someone bugging you? This freezing spell is designed to help prevent toxic people from bothering or contacting you anymore. Maybe there is someone who copies your ideas or work, or someone who you want to avoid but they won't take no for an answer. Try giving them the cold shoulder and freeze them out with some stone cold magic.

You will need:

- A zip-lock freezer bag
- Water
- A freezer
- A piece of paper
- A marker pen

1. Pour water into the zip-lock bag until it is about two-thirds full. (When water freezes, it expands, so don't fill the bag to the top.)

2. Use the marker pen to write a clear, personal intention on the piece of paper. For example: 'I hereby bind X (insert name of the person that's bothering you) to stop them from criticising me in front of my other friends', or 'I refuse to let X bring me down and interfere with my happiness any longer'.

3. Fold the paper three times and say: "I hereby freeze X and bind them from bothering me again".

4. As you do this, focus all your energy and attention on imagining the person removing themselves from your life or imagine their words no longer having any negative power over you.

5. Put the paper into the bag, seal it, and put it into a freezer. Leave it there as long as you need to.

6. Once the problem is sorted, you can, if you wish (and if you need space in the freezer!), remove the bag from the freezer and thaw out the water. Bury the paper in soil in a garden or plant pot and pour the water from the bag over the spot where the paper is buried.

7. You can use this spell as often as you feel the need to in order to ensure your home is safe and protected.

Simple Shield Protection Spell

The power of your mind can be considered one of your greatest assets. One of the best ways to ensure you are mentally and physically protected is by casting a shielding spell. It creates a powerful shield of safety and protection around you, filled with positive and uplifting energy.

This protection spell is simple to do and you do not need any ingredients for it, but it does require a lot of focus and belief, so ensure you pick a time to do it when you're not feeling stressed or distracted.

1. Sit comfortably and quietly on the floor, in a space and at a time you know you will not be disturbed. Centre yourself and find a place of calmness and serenity by taking seven deep breaths, in through the nose and out through the mouth. Visualise yourself drawing energy up from the ground below you and into your body with each inhalation.

2. Now imagine that energy spreading out from your body into the space around you. Visualise it expanding to form a bubble that you can see around you. You should be able to see it like a giant soap bubble that surrounds your entire being.

3. Close your eyes but make sure you can still 'see' the protective bubble around you. It is white and its surface is reflective, like the surface of a mirror. Anything harmful that comes your way will bounce off this surface. It won't be able to reach you.

4. Ensure the shield of protection stays in place with the following words: "I invoke this shield of safety. No harm or threats can reach me while I am safe within its magical protection".

Make a Protection Spell Jar

With its tough, spiky leaves, holly seems to be a plant destined to be used for protection. They are evergreen, so can withstand any weather, and provide shelter to hedgehogs and other small mammals. In this spell jar, you will use holly to give you something concrete to focus on and to remind you to feel safe, powerful and protected.

You will need:

- A glass jar with lid
- A holly leaf
- Some parsley
- A black hematite crystal
- A black obsidian crystal
- A smoky quartz crystal

- Pine needles or pine cones
- Garlic
- Salt
- A piece of paper
- A pen
- A black candle

1. Collect all of your items together on your altar before you start. Don't stress if you don't have all three of the crystals listed above. You can use any protective crystals you like.

2. Start adding the ingredients to the jar one at a time. Take your time doing this and as you add an item to the jar, think about what it represents and how it relates to your intention in casting the spell.

3. Finally, write down your wishes and intentions on the paper. For example: 'I am always safe in my home', or 'In my home I am shielded from harm'. Then fold it and put it in the jar.

4. Light the candle, screw the lid on the jar and seal it with molten wax. As you do so, state your intention out loud or in your head, and enjoy the reassuring feeling of security and safety washing over you.

5. When you're done, put your jar somewhere you'll see it often to remind you of your intention. You could keep the jar on your altar, beside your bed, on a windowsill, by your door or any place that feels right to you.

A Spell for Courage and Strength

This is a spell you can turn to any time you need a boost of strength or courage, and it'll work better than listening to any power ballad. But to max out its potential, try casting this spell on a Tuesday (as it's a good day for spells related to strength, vitality and courage) or on a Sunday (a good day for spells relating to personal growth and physical strength). Try to get as many of the herbs and spices listed below as you can, but don't worry too much; you can also use other ingredients that are connected to power, strength and protection from your pantry.

You will need:

- A dragon's blood incense stick
- A red candle
- Clove essential oil
- Cayenne pepper
- Chilli pepper
- Garlic
- Coriander
- A small drawstring bag or pouch

1. Put some cayenne pepper, chilli pepper, garlic and coriander into the small bag or pouch. Hold the bag in your hands and charge it with your intention. For example: "I will be strong. I will be brave".

2. Rub the clove essential oil all over the entire candle to charge it.

3. Light the candle. The candle is red to symbolise courage and the clove oil is for protection.

4. Use the candle flame to light the dragon's blood incense stick. Dragon's blood is a bright red resin obtained from a plant that is commonly used for protection.

5. Gaze into the flame of your candle and hold the bag of herbs in one hand. Breathe in and out slowly, imagining that you are inhaling courage and exhaling doubt and fear. You can repeat your intention here three times, either out loud or in your head. As you do so, try to feel your body being permeated with strength and courage.

6. When you're done, put the bag under your pillow and let its powers inspire you as you sleep.

A Spell to Lift and Protect Your Powers

Do you ever wake up and feel like you just can't brave that day? Are there times when you feel completely devoid of energy? This is a spell to boost your feelings of empowerment. You can use it to feel more confident and powerful in your day-to-day life or to boost and protect your belief in your own magical abilities.

You will need:

- Your favourite crystal
- Four protective crystals, such as obsidian or black tourmaline
- A compass
- A white candle
- A bunch of sage
- A fireproof tray or plate

1. Gather the items required for the spell and place them on your altar. You could play some music that makes you feel strong and passionate and ready to achieve anything you put your mind to.

2. Next, place your protective crystals in the four corners of your room. Use the compass to align the crystals with the directions north, south, east and west to ensure energy comes to you from all directions.

3. Light the white candle and use its flame to burn the sage. When the sage is smouldering, put on the fireproof tray or plate.

4. Next, hold your favourite crystal in your hands, close your eyes and try to imagine energy flowing up from the earth and into your body. As you do this, repeat an affirmation three times to help make you feel empowered, such as: "I am magical. I am powerful. I am confident. I am strong".

5. Continue focusing on your affirmations while clasping your favourite crystal until you feel ready to seize the day.

6. To end the spell, thank the universe for giving you power and protection and blow out the candle.

SPELLS FOR LOVE AND SEX

Love is a little bit like magic. Both are all about possibilities – the possibilities of changing and enhancing your life. Both also require belief, courage and commitment! Love spells are among the most popular of all spells cast. And no wonder, as so many of us are looking for romance, love or even 'The One', or struggling with heartache and mending a broken heart.

Love boundaries

Love spells can help you find or improve loving relationships, but even the most powerful magic spells cannot force someone to fall in love with you. Love spells also need to be cast to manifest something that is within the realms of possibility. Any spell you perform needs to call upon a result that is reasonable and possible. In other words, you'll be wasting your time trying to cast a love spell on your favourite Hollywood celebrity! Love spells are mostly intended to be used to strengthen a connection with someone you already know and to help you enhance that connection. A spell cannot instantly make them turn up on your doorstep with a bunch of roses in hand. So, as well as casting love spells on someone you are interested in, you should also let them know how you feel in other ways, such as sending them a text or making the effort to stop for a casual chat when you see them. You also need to truly believe in your heart that the relationship can work. Positive intentions are key!

It's all about you

Even if you are looking for a spell to get the attention of someone you already vaguely know, it's still best to focus spells on yourself rather than on other people. For example, if what you need is to recover from a broken heart, casting a spell to get revenge on your ex might not work, while casting a spell to increase your self-love and worth might have more fruitful results. It's also helpful to be open-minded when it comes to your intentions in a spell. So instead of asking for specific physical features in a partner, ask for a partner who makes you feel safe, wanted or happy.

As with almost all the spells you'll ever perform, the most important thing is not what you do, it's about how well you can focus, believe in and concentrate on your intentions. It's not the crystals you choose or the candle you light, but the openness of your heart and sincerity of your intention that you put into your love spells that will make them work. A little bit of patience doesn't go amiss either, as a love spell can take any length of time to work. It's hard to say how long the manifestation of a spell might take. But remember, if you're watching the clock and getting frustrated that Cupid's arrow isn't flying fast enough to its target, then you're diminishing the power needed to make your spell succeed.

GOOD TO KNOW

There are many different reasons a love spell can miss its target, but if they really aren't working for you then maybe hit the pause button and have a think about what could be going wrong. Maybe you're not ready for new love, perhaps because you still haven't got over a broken heart? Or maybe you always have the same issues that prevent you opening up to a partner? Sometimes it can help to talk to a friend to work out if there are any deeper issues that are getting in the way of you finding love. Then again, maybe it's just not the right time for love for you. Take time instead to focus on work and other friendships, and try again later when the time is more auspicious for you.

Manifest New Love

There are some love spells that you can do that require no ingredients at all. Instead they depend on the magical power of manifestation. This love spell is designed to help you meet a potential partner or draw you closer to someone with whom you already have some kind of a connection.

1. First, check your lunar calendar. The best time to cast love spells is on a Friday because it's linked to Venus, the goddess of love, and on the day of a new moon, because these are symbolic of new beginnings.

2. On the appointed evening, settle yourself in a quiet room where you won't be disturbed and where you can fully relax and concentrate.

3. Set your intention. This is the most important part of manifestation, so be clear in your mind of what you'd like to achieve. Make your intention as specific as possible. The more clear and concise, the better. So, instead of saying, "I want to meet the partner of my dreams", focus on someone you already know and like, or come up with a detailed idea of what that person would be like, such as their personality, characteristics and values.

4. When you're sure your intention is clear, focus on thinking about the person or type of person you wish to get closer to. Imagine being with that person, and imagine being in a loving relationship with them. Try to empty your mind of everything else, aside from the mental images you've created of the two of you together. Believe in the transformational power of your love and energy.

5. Repeat the manifestation once a month, ideally on the night of a full moon.

6. In order to see positive results, remember that while manifesting can help you turn your dreams into reality, you do need to help fate along by putting yourself out there and being ready and available to welcome new love.

Romance Spell

When you have an infatuation with someone but they don't seem to have noticed it yet, this spell can help you feel love and romance in the air and project the idea of the connection into the universe. With the right intentions, it should bring you and the object of your affection closer together.

You will need:

- A bathtub filled with water
- A glass of milk
- Some rose petals
- Your favourite essential oils
- A rose quartz crystal
- Four new (unused) pink candles

1. First, take the time to give your bath a really good scrub. It should be cleaned and cleansed so the ingredients can work effectively.

2. Fill the bathtub with hot water and play some gentle background music to enhance the romantic atmosphere you are trying to build.

3. Stand a pink candle on each corner of the bathtub and light each one.

4. Pour the glass of milk, rose petals and essential oils into the water. Place the rose quartz crystal in last, after charging it with your intention. Think about what you want your ingredients to help you achieve in order to fill them with magical energy.

5. Then, get into the bath, close your eyes and relax. As you do so, be actively aware of the warm water flowing over your body, the spellbinding scents of the oils and the romantic music.

6. Now visualise yourself and the person you are attracted to as a couple. Picture yourselves together, being happy and in love. Try to avoid thinking about anything else other than your intentions.

7. After soaking in your bath, collect the rose petals and dry them out. Keep them in your bedroom on a dish beside your bed.

Saffron Spell for Seduction

This is a spell to be performed in the evening. It helps you spice up your sex life and inflame a burning desire between you and your partner. It is designed to rekindle the spark in an existing relationship or to bring even more passion into a new one, and it works by increasing your sexual desire and someone's sexual desire towards you.

You will need:

- A red candle
- Red items of clothing
- Saffron
- A bowl or dish
- A sachet bag

1. Before you start this spell, dress in red. This can be something as simple as a red scarf, or you could go all out with red underwear and a full red outfit. You can even add some red lipstick or nail varnish for good measure.

2. Put the saffron in the dish in front of the candle. Saffron has been used since ancient times as a natural aphrodisiac and modern research suggests that it does indeed boost sexual stamina and desire.

3. Turn off the lights and light the red candle.

4. Sit comfortably and quietly while staring into the candle flame, concentrating on visualising sexual encounters, either real or fantasy, that have brought you the most pleasure in the past. Lose yourself in these sensual memories and focus on how your body feels when you're reminiscing on those times. This spell will really only work if you give yourself up to these feelings in both your body and soul.

5. Allow yourself plenty of time to enjoy those feelings. When you're finished, blow out the candle and put the saffron in the sachet. (You can make a sachet bag by sewing two small sheets of muslin together. If sewing isn't your thing, you can buy one from your nearest craft shop.)

6. Tuck the saffron sachet into your underwear drawer or your pillowcase and wait for the passion to ignite!

Ribbon Spell

Is there someone out there you have a crush on but who doesn't seem to know you exist? This spell should help to bring you and your dream lover together. We suggest using two red candles here, but you can use any two objects that make an obvious pair – one to represent you and one to represent your crush. For example, you can use salt and pepper shakers or a pair of gloves, earrings or slippers – whichever you most connect with.

You will need:

- Two red candles
- Some rose petals
- Oils and herbs including patchouli oil, nutmeg, rosemary and camomile
- A bowl (ideally red or pink)
- Pink or red ribbon

1. Place two red candles in front of you on your altar, one to represent you and the other for your crush.

2. Next, mix the oils and herbs in a bowl to bind the ingredients together. (Choosing a red or pink bowl can intensify the romantic or passionate nature of the magic.) The warm scent of patchouli oil cultivates deep, lasting relationships and including nutmeg in love spells helps to dispel the occasional awkwardness of blossoming love. Rosemary has a protective vibe, to guard yourself from getting hurt in new relationships. Camomile is known as a lucky flower, so it's ideal for helping you to attract a new lover.

3. Anoint the first candle with the mixture, then the other candle, visualising yourself and your love interest together.

4. Take the ribbon and tie the two candles loosely together, leaving a good length of ribbon in between.

5. Every morning for a week, untie the ribbon, move the candles a bit closer together, and then retie the knots. Do this until they're touching.

6. Then, leave them tied together for another seven days. By this time, or not too long after, you should have a chance encounter with the target of your affection.

A Spell to Sweeten a Relationship

Are you and your partner having issues? Do you have difficulty communicating, trusting each other or getting stuck in a cycle of arguing about petty things? Then this is the spell for you. This honey jar spell helps to sweeten an existing relationship. Sticky honey is often used in magic spells for bringing two things together. The bee is a symbol of fertility and honey is known to create balance. It can bind a couple who find themselves in a rocky patch.

You will need:

- A jar of honey
- A piece of paper
- A pen
- A boiled kettle
- A mug
- A teaspoon

1. Write the name of your loved one on the paper three times. The number three is significant here. For ancient philosophers, the number three was considered to be the perfect number; the number of harmony, wisdom and understanding. It's also linked to Jupiter, the planet of joy, abundance, success, good fortune and wisdom.

2. Next, write down your intention. This has to be expressed very clearly if the spell is to work. Be plain and concise. For example: 'My love and I will listen more carefully to each other's needs'.

3. Then, fold the paper three times, making sure that it fits neatly into the honey jar.

4. Take a spoonful of honey out of the jar and use it to make yourself some tea with freshly boiled water. While you drink and enjoy this sweet tea, repeat this affirmation: "As I take this tea, you'll be this sweet to me". You can say this in your head or out loud. You can also choose some words of your own to repeat at this stage.

5. Once you finish your tea, there is one thing left to do. Put the lid back on your honey jar and bury the jar somewhere safe. Ideally, find somewhere near some flowering plants or herbs, or at the bottom of a plant pot, fully submerged.

A Spell to Help You Get Over a Break Up

While falling in love can make you feel like you're walking on air, breaking up can sometimes send you crashing down again. Splitting up with a partner, whether it's a long term or a fairly new relationship, can leave you feeling bruised and sad. This spell can help to lift some of that pain and help you start to heal that wounded heart.

You will need:

- A smudge stick made from rosemary and sage
- A small black candle
- A candleholder
- An uncooked, uncracked, clean and room temperature egg
- A pair of scissors or knife

1. First, light the rosemary and sage smudge stick and then wave the smoke through your room to fill your space with positive energy. Take your time to do this slowly and rhythmically, taking in the smell and cleansing properties of the smouldering herbs.

2. Next, carefully cut the black candle in two and put the top part in a candleholder. Set it on your altar and light it. (You need a small candle because you want it to burn for a short time, just the length of time it takes to complete the spell.)

3. As the candle burns, take the uncooked egg and gently rub it over your body, taking extra time and focus over the heart area. Eggs are a symbol of life and they can draw negative energy out of your body. The egg should soak up your sadness and take it inside its shell. Think of the egg as a sort of psychic vacuum cleaner!

4. When the candle has burnt out, take it and the egg and dispose of them in a bin or bury them outside in the earth.

Note: It's natural to feel weary after this spell. Carrying sadness and negative energy is tiring, and letting it go is tiring too. You should feel better and have more positive energy within a day or two.

A Binding Spell

Happy in your relationship but every time you mention the word 'exclusive' your partner runs for the hills? Are you ready to move from 'it's complicated' to 'in a relationship' status? Perhaps what you need is a binding spell. These spells can prove effective when using a photograph of your beloved, and you only need a few simple objects you can find at home to do it.

You will need:

- A photo of your beloved
- A photo of yourself
- A piece of parchment paper
- A pen
- Black thread or ribbon
- A small pink candle
- Rose oil
- A toothpick
- A fireproof tray or plate

1. Take the toothpick and use it to gently carve your name and the name of the other person on one side of the pink candle. Then carve an image of a simple key on the other side of the candle.

2. Dress the candle by covering it with rose oil. As you dress your candle, say the words that describe your intention, for example: "With this pink candle, I'll infuse my relationship with commitment". Light your candle and repeat your intentions.

3. Next, write both your name and your lover's on the parchment paper, then carefully pour melting wax from your lit candle over the paper. The key thing here is to make sure that you cover both names with the wax.

4. Take the two photos and wrap them in the parchment paper. Tie the black thread or ribbon around the paper parcel with the photos inside. As the candle burns down, focus your mind on your intentions and desires.

5. After the candle has burnt down, put the parcel of photos under your bed for a week. Then, take it out, burn it carefully (such as on a fireproof tray outdoors), and dispose of the ashes.

Self–love Spell Jar

It's never good to need the love of another person to feel worthy or secure. You'll never be satisfied just with love from someone else. One of the most important forms of love is self-love. Loving yourself means taking time to look after yourself, being kind to yourself and owning your thoughts and opinions. When you love yourself, you radiate positivity. You give off happy, confident vibes that act like a powerful magnet, attracting other people to you. When you truly love and respect yourself, you're also better able to trust your feelings and decisions, so you'll know who is right for you when they come along.

You will need:

- A glass jar with lid
- Rose petals
- Lavender
- Pink Himalayan salt
- Lemon peel
- Sandalwood
- A rose quartz or clear quartz crystal
- A pink candle
- A piece of paper
- A pen

1. Write some self-love affirmations or self-love quotes on the piece of paper. Write them as beautifully and clearly as you can. This could include phrases like: 'I accept myself for all of my beautiful and not-so-cool quirks and qualities', or 'I believe that I'm capable of achieving and creating the life that I deserve and dream of', or 'I'm going to spend time with people who support, encourage and motivate me to be the best version of myself'.

2. Then, place the ingredients into the jar. Arrange them so they look appealing and enjoy taking your time doing this.

3. Light the pink candle, screw the lid on the jar and seal it with molten wax.

4. Stand your self-love spell jar on your altar or bedside table, or somewhere else you will see it often, so it can remind you to practise more acts of self-love.

Apple Love Spell

The humble apple has been steeped in rich symbolism throughout history as having magical, life-giving powers. When it comes to witchcraft and magic, the apple historically has strong associations with love. Use this spell to call forth a lover into your life, to add romance or passion to an existing relationship, or cast it on yourself for self-love. This spell can be performed at any time, but is especially effective during apple harvest season in autumn.

You will need:

- An apple
- A small pink candle
- Some ground cinnamon
- Some sugar
- A flat plate or dish
- A knife
- A toothpick
- Essential oils, such as patchouli, rose or ylang-ylang

1. Cut about 2 cm off the top of the apple and put this to one side of your altar for later.

2. From the remaining part of the apple, cut a large slice so one side is still covered in peel and the other is raw apple.

3. Use the toothpick to carve your intentions onto the raw side of the apple slice. For example, you could write: 'Love and affection', 'Love for myself' or 'Romance and passion'.

4. Next, add some cinnamon and sugar to a flat dish for taste. Then, dunk the carved side of the apple slice into the cinnamon and sugar mix.

5. Add some essential oil to the cinnamon and sugar mix. Then, roll the candle in the mix.

6. Remove the stem from the apple top, if it has one, and carve a hole in the centre that is big enough to hold the candle.

7. Place the candle in the apple and set it on a safe, flat surface, ideally on your altar. Light the candle and focus on its flame and your wishes as you repeat the words carved on the apple slice.

8. Eat the apple slice, and blow out the candle when you are ready.

Bringing Back an Ex Spell

This spell only has a chance of working if you cast it during the night of a waxing moon. It's also a spell to try with caution. Think carefully if it's the right thing to do. Is there a valid reason you broke up? Are you missing that particular person or do you just miss being in a relationship? Consider this fully before proceeding with the spell.

You will need:

- A red candle
- A candleholder
- A photo of just your ex
- A piece of paper
- A pencil
- A spoon
- Honey

1. On the evening of a waxing moon, sit your red candle in a candleholder on your altar and light it. Sit looking at the candle for three minutes with your attention totally focused on its flickering flame.

2. Then, look at the photograph of your ex for three minutes. Visualise your memories together – all the good times you had – and visualise the two of you getting back together. The more vivid your mental images are, the better.

3. Next, write your name and your ex's name on the piece of paper. Draw a circle around both of your names, so both names are inside the same circle.

4. Dip the spoon in the honey and gently drizzle it over the circle of names on the paper. As you do this, repeat this incantation out loud or in your head:

   "With this spell, I call you back to me".

5. Put the spoon down and get into a comfortable sitting position and breathe deeply in through your nose and slowly out through your mouth three times, then three times again. Once you feel fully calm and relaxed, blow out the candle.

6. Rip the paper with the names on it into small pieces and bury them in soil.

7. You can repeat this spell over the three nights of the waxing moon, using the same candle as the first night, for maximum impact.

SPELLS FOR WEALTH AND PROSPERITY

If you've turned to this section of the book looking for a simple spell that will help you win the lottery and become filthy rich overnight, you'll be disappointed to find that you've come to the wrong place. If it were that easy, witches all over the world would be drowning in cash! The money and prosperity spells you'll find here are intended to help you find a level of wealth, prosperity and success that equates to financial security, wellbeing and good career opportunities. In fact, some witches feel they should only perform magic spells when they're really in dire need of money and strapped for cash, not just because they want more, more, more.

Money matters

Before embarking on these spells, have a think about your attitude to and relationship with money, and be honest with yourself. Are you someone who tends to waste money? Wasting anything, including money, creates negative energy. If you continue to splash your cash on stuff you don't need, that's going to make it very hard to conjure up abundance and wealth, no matter how hard you try. On the other hand, worrying about money all the time and holding on to all of your cash tightly will not bring you happiness either. Like so much of life, it's all about balance – in this case, striking a balance between saving and spending. It's also a state of mind. Try to make your thoughts about money more positive. For example, on occasions when money is tight and you worry yourself with thoughts such as, "I can't possibly afford that!", change your mindset to "I'd rather not spend my money on that right now", or "My funds are just a little low at the moment".

Top Tips

Here are some tips for taking charge of your finances before you set up your spells. Some of it might sound obvious, but it's always good to remind ourselves what matters most.

- Only spend what you can afford. Don't spend what you don't have. Try to avoid getting into too much debt. The longer you take to pay a debt, the more you'll end up owing.

- Cut down on wasteful spending. We all need to exercise a little self-control when we're shopping. Think before you buy!

- Take some time to set a budget. This involves working out what you've got coming in and what's going out, and making sure that you can afford all your bills and necessities.

- Track your spending. Once you've set yourself a budget, try to keep an eye on where you're spending your money. Download an app that allows you to keep track of your purchases, with each transaction put into a particular category. You can then quickly and easily see where your money is being spent, and where you might be able to make some savings.

- After you've got your budget pinned down, you can start to put some cash aside for unexpected emergencies. The idea of an 'emergency fund' might seem extreme, but it's a way of making sure you've got some money on hand for an unplanned expense without falling into debt.

So, are you ready to manifest some money and make a dash for the cash? Just remember three things. Firstly, take control of your ideas about money and any negative spending habits. Secondly, be patient. As with any spell casting, you cannot control how long spells and manifestations will take. Finally, have faith in yourself and your ability to bring your dreams and desires to reality.

Passing Tests Spell

Sometimes, the thing that stands between us and prosperity and wealth is an exam, job interview or test of some kind. This simple spell is designed to help you pass a test with flying colours. It helps your focus and concentration and it can be your good luck charm. (Of course, this will only work if you've also revised for the test or prepared for the interview properly too!)

You will need:

- A yellow candle
- 1 incense stick or essential oil (such as lemon, lavender, rosemary, cinnamon or peppermint)
- Your study books or course material
- A piece of paper
- A pencil

1. First, light your chosen incense or burn your essential oil. Place your hands on your study books. Take three long, deep breaths. Relax and have a positive attitude. Meditating for a few minutes and absorbing the cleansing scent of the oils will help to ground you.

2. Draw a sketch of the Sun on the piece of paper. This image can be as big or small, decorative or simple as you like. Just think about what you're drawing and be conscious of the way the pencil moves across the paper.

3. Light the yellow candle. As it burns, stare into the flame and chant this spell:

   "I open my heart to the power of the Sun,
   I see deep into the glow of its light,
   with its bright focus and wisdom,
   I can pass this test".

4. Imagine basking in the Sun's light and feeling it clear your mind. You're invoking the Sun's energy to give you strength, focus and memory to help you pass the exam.

5. Meditate for a few minutes.

6. When you're done, blow out the candle but keep the drawing of the Sun. You will need to take this with you to be your lucky charm for the exam, perhaps in a pocket or bag or where you can see it on a desk or table.

Money Spell Jar

In this spell, you're going to fill a spell jar with tokens that will invoke the energy you need to succeed. But, don't forget to pair your spell with action. To get the most out of the energy you're trying to attract into your life using your spell jar, you need to take action to achieve your goal as well. So, if you want to achieve more success or earn more money, you've got to put yourself out there and find a new job, a new course, or talk to people who can help you. Doing this spell on a new or full moon is ideal for maximum potential.

You will need:

- A glass jar with lid
- A jade crystal
- A green aventurine crystal
- Ginger
- Thyme

- A selection of seeds
- Rice or flour
- A piece of paper
- A pen
- A green, gold or yellow candle

1. First, take a few cleansing breaths or cleanse the space around your altar in your preferred way.

2. Place your items in the jar one at a time. You really need to do this mindfully and with intention, thinking about what each object represents and how it might help you achieve your goal.

3. Write down your intention on the paper and place it in the jar. You could write something like: 'Success and prosperity are coming my way', or 'Money will be mine'.

4. Light a green, gold or yellow candle (colours which symbolise success and prosperity) and state your intention out loud. As you state your intentions, imagine what it will be like when they come true.

5. Screw the lid on the jar and seal it with molten wax from your candle.

6. When you've finished the ritual, put your jar somewhere you'll see it often, to remind you of your intention.

Bay Leaf Money Spell

This spell will help you to attract money and prosperity. Bay leaves are symbols of success and achieving goals and they were treasured by the Roman gods, who wore sprigs of bay as crowns to represent their high status. In the past, heroes were also given a wreath made of bay (also called laurel) leaves.

You will need:

- A dried bay leaf
- A marker pen
- A pair of tweezers
- A match or lighter
- A metal, fireproof bowl
- A white candle (optional)

1. Lay the dried bay leaf on a flat surface, such as your altar. Use the marker pen to write a word such as 'Abundance', 'Prosperity' or 'Wealth' as clearly as you can on the upper side of the bay leaf.

2. After you've written your word, begin to draw small currency signs all over the rest of the space on the bay leaf, until that surface of the bay leaf is almost entirely covered with markings.

3. Pick up the bay leaf by the stem end with your tweezers (so you don't damage the leaf or your markings). Hold the leaf over your metal bowl and with your other hand, light the bay leaf at the tip (opposite to the tweezers). As the bay leaf catches fire and burns, state your wishes and intentions. Or you could chant something like:

"Money come and money grow
   money's mine, so let it flow".

4. When the leaf has turned to ashes, you can sprinkle the ashes onto the top of a white candle and keep it on your altar space. Or, you can blow them into the wind out of your door or window, to send your wishes into the universe to be heard.

Money Bowl Spell

This spell is used to bring forth money to your home or ask for a pay rise. It is important to choose or borrow a suitable bowl for this spell. A tin or copper bowl would be ideal as these metals are associated with money, trading, prosperity and success. A green or gold coloured bowl would also be a plus because these colours are strongly associated with money and fortune. If you can't get your hands on one of these, try to use a clear glass bowl, to keep your intentions clear.

You will need:

- A bowl
- Small items that represent wealth and money, such as a small money purse
- Coins or cash
- One or two crystals (such as citrine, aventurine or pyrite)
- A small green or gold candle
- Essential oils such as bergamot or eucalyptus
- A piece of paper
- A pen
- A sage smudge stick

1. First, use your smudge stick to smoke cleanse all of the items that you've chosen to add into your bowl, and place the bowl on your altar.

2. Then, write your intentions on the paper, as if they have already happened. For example: 'I have all the money I need', or 'My credit card is paid off'.

3. Put all your objects, except the candle, oil, pen and paper, into the bowl one by one. State your intention as you add each object.

4. Add a couple of drops of essential oil. Light the candle.

5. Finally, fold the paper with your intention written on it and add this to the bowl.

6. Place the bowl near your front door to attract wealth to you. Keep adding to your money bowl every few days with other objects that represent wealth and prosperity to you.

7. You can keep blowing out the candle and burning it again on your altar until it is used up.

Money Attraction Spell

This is a very simple spell to attract money into your life that requires very few ingredients. The green candle represents money and the white candle represents yourself. Because of the simplicity of this spell, it's super important to state the affirmations with deep conviction and concentration, as that is where the power of this spell (and many other spells) resides.

You will need:

- A green candle
- A white candle
- An essential oil of your choosing (preferably cinnamon, sweet orange or peppermint)

1. The first order of business is to charge the two candles. Charging the candles is vital, as it instils the objects with your magical intent. To do this, hold the candles in your hands and repeat an affirmation such as: "Money will flow my way", or whatever intention suits your purpose.

2. Put a few drops of your chosen essential oil onto each candle. This oil will help to set your intention.

3. Set the candles about 18 cm apart on your altar. At the same time every day for nine days, repeat the below or a similar affirmation of your own creation:

    "Money and riches come to me,
    bring me prosperity,
    three times three.
    This I wish for, let it be.
    Bring me money,
    three times three".

4. As you repeat this affirmation, conjure up a mental image of money flowing to you. Visualise the prosperity that you desire. At the same time, you should gently move the white candle 2 cm closer to the green candle. Don't move the green candle. After nine days, the two candles meet and your spell is done.

5. Once your money attraction spell is complete, you can carry on with your day-to-day life with the belief that your finances will improve in the future.

Necklace for Success Spell

In this spell, you will fill a tiny, corked bottle or jar to hang on a necklace with herbs and spices from your kitchen that will help you attract money. You can buy small corked bottles on cord necklaces very cheaply online. Allspice is associated with money and good fortune and ginger calls forth prosperity and success. Nutmeg works well for attracting luck and money. Cloves were once so expensive that only the very wealthy could afford them, so they are historically associated with wealth.

You will need:

- A tiny, corked bottle or jar to hang on a necklace
- Allspice
- Ginger
- Ground or whole cloves
- Nutmeg
- Ground cinnamon
- A small funnel or folded paper
- A tiny piece or shavings of tiger's eye (or clear quartz)
- Bergamot essential oil
- A gold or yellow candle

1. Open your bottle/jar and use the small funnel or folded paper to help you pour some allspice, ginger, cloves and nutmeg into it. These herbs and spices form the base layer of your spell.

2. Now, hold a tiny piece of tiger's eye or the shavings of tiger's eye in your hand and charge it with your intentions. Then, add it to the bottle/jar. Tiger's eye is good for luck and will add power to your spell.

3. Add some ground cinnamon, a botanical that not only helps you attract money and prosperity, but also intensifies the properties of the other herbs.

4. Sprinkle in a few drops of bergamot oil to attract success and encourage prosperity. It will also make your money spell necklace fragrant and more powerful.

5. Light a gold or a yellow candle as these colours correspond with luck and good fortune. Cork the bottle/jar and carefully seal it with wax from the candle.

6. Wear the necklace or keep it by you to work its magic and bring you prosperity.

Find a New Job Spell

This spell will help you get the job you desire and soon you should have enough money in the bank to pay all those bills and hopefully fund some of the fun extras you've been daydreaming about!

You will need:

- A piece of green paper
- A gold pen
- Three mint leaves
- A teaspoon of dried sage
- One gold or silver candle in a candleholder

1. First, draw a large pentagram (a powerful symbol made up of a circle with a five-pointed star inside it) in the centre of the piece of paper with your gold pen. Green and gold colours bring luck and money.

2. You now need to write the word 'JOB' in the centre of the star. Before putting pen to paper, make sure that the star is pointing up, not down, and don't make the word too big as you need room to add other words to the pentagram too.

3. In the space around 'JOB', write some other words describing your ideal job. Do you want an office-based or home-based role, outdoor work, or full or part-time work?

4. Rip the mint leaves into pieces and put them and the dried sage into the pentagram.

5. Sit the candleholder on top of the herbs and light the candle. Then repeat these words:

   "Nature and the universe, I call on you
   to find me a job I'll love to do,
   offer me work to pay my bills,
   and all my needs and wishes are fulfilled".

6. Wait for the candle to finish burning. Then remove the candle and carry the paper with the herbs resting on it to an open window. Blow the herbs out into the air to carry your intentions into the universe.

7. You should soon find the job that you've been hoping for!